Ordinary Dogs, *Extraordinary* Friendships

Stories of Loyalty, Courage, and Compassion

Pam Flowers

ALASKA NORTHWEST BOOKS®

Library of Congress Cataloging-in-Publication Data
Flowers, Pam.
    Ordinary dogs, extraordinary friendships : stories of loyalty, courage, and compassion / Pam Flowers.
        pages cm
Audience: 8-12.
Includes bibliographical references and index.
    ISBN 978-0-88240-916-0 (pbk. : alk. paper)
    ISBN 978-0-88240-978-8 (hardbound)
    ISBN 978-0-88240-967-2 (e-book) 1. Dogs—
Juvenile literature. I. Title.

    SF426.5.F62 2013
    636.7—dc23

                                            2013017986

Editor: Michelle McCann
Illustrations: Jason Baskin
Designer: Vicki Knapton

Published by Alaska Northwest Books Press®
An imprint of Graphic Arts Books
P.O. Box 56118
Portland, Oregon 97238-6118
503-254-5591
www.graphicartsbooks.com

To my dog, Amy,
friend of Chinook,
mother of Douggie,
grandmother of Alice, Matt, and Robert,
great grandmother of Sojo, Anna, and Roald,
distant cousin of Lucy, Jocko, and Ellie,
and my best friend for sixteen years.

CONTENTS

Introduction

Like a lot of families, mine acquired a series of pet dogs over the years. I loved every one of those dogs. But the one I remember most was a friendly German shepherd named Lady. I think we got her when I was in the third grade.

Every day as I set out for school, Lady would sit on the porch and watch as I walked away. But I know she didn't stay there very long because, after a few minutes, I could see her peeking out from behind a house along the way. Then she would lower her ears and slink across the open space to the next house and the next. When I got to school, Lady would turn around and head home. And every day after school, she would be waiting for me on the porch as though she had never gone anywhere. I think Lady thought she was getting away with something and probably thought it was fun.

We spent a lot of time hiking together during summers and skiing in the winters. Mostly, we enjoyed just hanging around with each other. Growing up, Lady was my best friend.

Since Lady I've shared my life with many dogs. I've traveled thousands of miles with dog teams, hiked trails all over North America with dogs, and always have at least one dog with me when I drive anywhere. I can't imagine life without dogs.

What I have come to understand about dogs is that they are smarter than most people realize and that we humans have a lot in common with them. We live in packs, work together, and play together. And dogs, like people, feel sadness and disappointment, seek kindness and affection, and need a purpose to be happy.

Dogs have a remarkable ability to take what life hands them and respond in inspiring ways. By watching them I have learned a lot about compassion, loyalty, and forgiveness. In the Arctic, when I was afraid, dogs helped me find more courage than I ever knew I had. I have seen dogs show a sense of fairness and strength of character that leaves me in awe. By their example, dogs have made me a better person and they have made the world a better place for all of us.

Because dogs have added so much to my life, I have developed a passion for telling stories about amazing things my dogs have done. I selected the stories in this book because they show my dogs demonstrating these character traits.

Every one of these dogs deserves the respect that I hope shows through in these pages.

You'll meet:

Douggie (pronounced DUG-ee),

Amy and Chinook (shi-NOOK),

Hank and Jocko (JOK-o),

Sojo (SO-jo) and Roald (ROL-d),

Lucy and Anna (AH-nah),

and Ellie and Kaiya (KI-yah).

Any dog you meet has many positive character traits. They're there—you just have to take the time to look. And when you see those traits, you'll know that every dog is worthy of your respect.

1

AMY IS MISSING

We have all heard amazing stories in the news about a dog that knew something was wrong with a family member and tried to help. There's the dog that knew someone was going to have a seizure and went for help. The dog that saw a toddler was wandering onto the street and herded the little boy back to safety.

This is the story about the day my pet dog, Amy, went missing. The dogs in my team knew something was wrong, but they were all tied to their houses and so couldn't do much to help Amy. But they found a simple and powerful way to help me as I searched for her during that terrible time.

Amy was my best friend and she occupied a unique place in my world. Amy was the only sled dog I ever knew who wanted nothing to do with pulling a sled. She was content to lounge around in front of my cabin and was seldom tied to her house. My sled dogs were tied up most of the time and you might think they would be jealous of her freedom. But Amy was too clever to let that happen. The first thing she did every morning was walk around and pay a visit to each dog. She would sniff everyone good morning, wag her tail, and play a little before moving on to the next dog. She never showed any favorites and generally kept everyone happy. You might say she was the mayor of the dog lot.

Amy devoted her afternoons to me. I would head off to hike some nearby trail and she would tag along. She made a fine companion, never straying out of sight and always waiting patiently whenever I stopped to examine some interesting plant. Amy was beautiful, about the size of her German shepherd father, and she had the lush, tan coat of her collie mother. I often used this time alone with Amy to practice giving her commands. She would keep those golden brown eyes of hers focused on my right hand. With a simple flick of my wrist or motion of my hand, she would sit, stay, lie down, or come. If I wanted her to move out of my way, I simply had to say, "Amy, let's go," and she would move. Amy was the smartest dog I ever knew.

One spring morning I walked out of my cabin clutching a bunch of dog harnesses. There was just enough mushy snow left on the ground to make one final run with my dog team.

Because I didn't want Amy chasing us when my team and I went sledding, I usually tied her off to her doghouse while we were gone. On this particular morning Amy was nowhere to be seen. I wasn't worried, however, because I knew she would hear the dogs barking and come running home to watch the excitement. But when it came time to leave on our run, Amy still hadn't come back. I still wasn't worried because she had done this before and had always come home.

I was sure she would be there waiting when we returned.

An hour later, as we sledded back into the dog yard, I was surprised that Amy hadn't come home. I unharnessed the dogs and they curled up beside their houses to take a nap while I headed off to find Amy. We lived out in the country where there were lots of trails but I knew her favorite places. Most likely she had followed the narrow trail that led over a hill behind my cabin. The trail went through the forest for about a mile, crossed a railroad track, and ended at a snow-bank beside a gravel road. Since Amy seldom went all the way to the road, I figured it wouldn't take long to find her.

Just before reaching the gravel road, I came to where a creek runs beside part of the trail and then flows under a rail-road trestle. During the winter the creek is completely buried under snow and becomes invisible. But now that it was spring and the temperature had warmed, the snow cover had started to melt and sag over the creek. From a distance this saggy area appeared as a long, narrow, winding shadow and I could tell precisely where the creek flowed with its icy, cold water.

The creek's a pretty dangerous place right now, I thought. *There's no good reason for Amy to go to the creek so I'm not going to waste time trudging all the way over there.*

Every few minutes I'd stop, look around and call, "Amy. Amy, come," but there was no response. After an hour of searching, I walked home to see if she had come back. As I crested the hill, the dogs raised their heads, looked at me, and then went back to their naps. Amy was not there.

For five hours I searched, returning home every hour hoping to see Amy waiting by my front door. I hiked a moose trail and along the railroad tracks. No Amy. I studied the snow around a wild rabbit's den and searched by the compost pile. No Amy. I crawled under the porch and behind the woodpile. No Amy.

None of this was normal and by late afternoon the dogs had figured out that something was wrong. Tied to their houses, there was nothing they could do but Amy was their friend too and they found a way to show their concern. Every time I came over the little hill behind my cabin, they would all rise and stare at me in silence and then look past me as though they were expecting Amy to appear.

As the hours went by my stomach began to tighten with worry. In her entire life Amy had never stayed away this long. By evening I was panicked.

Where could she be? Why doesn't she come when I call her?

I saw grizzly tracks last week. Did that bear kill her? Did someone think she was a stray and shoot her?

I ran as fast as I could to the road, but there was no sign that Amy had ever been there. I racked my brain trying to think of where else to look. The sound of an engine interrupted my thoughts and I looked down the road to the crossing just as a huge snowplow roared past on the main highway. *No, Amy wouldn't go to the highway. She knows better. She would never do that.* But I had to consider that she might have gone there, that her body might by lying beside the highway, and I knew I had to go over there to look.

By the time I reached the highway, the sound of the truck's engine had faded into the distance. "Amy! Amy!" I shouted over and over but she didn't come. *This can't be happening. I cannot lose my best friend.*

My despair was wiped away by anger. *What's the matter with her? How could she run off like this?*

I slumped down onto the snowbank and started to cry. It wasn't Amy's fault, it was mine. *Why didn't I tie her up when I let her out this morning? Why didn't I go find her before I went mushing? Why didn't I take better care of her?*

There were no answers to these questions. I looked at my watch and realized it was one o'clock in the morning. I had now been searching for fourteen hours. I was exhausted and close to giving up. It was too dark to keep looking so I walked back along the road, climbed wearily over the snowbank, and followed the trail home. As I crested the hill, I expected the dogs would be curled up asleep inside their doghouses but they weren't. They were all sitting outside, looking toward the trail. As I trudged past them their gaze followed me to my cabin and then they turned their heads back toward the trail, silently waiting, waiting, waiting for Amy to return. It was as though they were saying, *Get some rest. We'll keep watch.*

I went to bed but sleep never came. I kept thinking about all those walks we had gone on together. I tried to remember every little side trail we had ever gone on, trying to figure out some place she could have wandered and maybe gotten herself lost. But Amy knew this area so well. It didn't seem possible that she could be lost.

The one thing I kept going back to in my mind again and again was the dogs watching the trail. *They know something,* I thought. *That's why they're not giving up.* I decided to use them as my guide for how long to search. As long as they didn't give up on their friend, neither would I.

By five o'clock it was light enough to start searching again so I put on my jacket and looked out the window. The dogs were all lying curled up outside their houses. Some seemed to have fallen asleep but everyone had their faces pointing toward the trail that led over the hill.

During the night a little snow had fallen and that brought a tiny flicker of hope. If Amy was around, her tracks would be obvious and I would soon find her. With new resolve, I set off over the hill in search of my friend.

Five hours later, having found not a single track and standing alone on that road in silence, the ugliest of all thoughts finally forced its way into my mind. *Amy is dead.*

She had probably wandered onto the highway and been struck by a passing vehicle. The best I could hope for was that I might find her body after the snow was all gone. Brokenhearted, I turned around and walked over to the snowbank.

What was it this time that made me climb the snowbank in a different spot? What magic lifted my feet? What force turned my eyes toward the creek at just the right moment? It *was* magic because from that one exact spot I could look straight up the creek along the narrow, deep trough, and straight into Amy's eyes!

There she was, standing belly deep in the icy, cold water. My eyes did not leave hers as my feet carried me splashing up the creek. When I reached her Amy was so weak she couldn't hold her head up to look at me but she managed the tiniest wag of her wet tail.

"Amy," I whispered softly. She looked so small, so haggard, so fragile. I gently wrapped my arms around her chest and heaved her upward. But the trough was five feet deep and I wasn't strong enough to shove her all the way to the top.

Amy's head and legs flopped uselessly. She was too weak to help pull herself up. I was losing my grip. Amy was slipping through my arms!

I had to do something quickly! I pressed my head tightly against her neck, pinning her head to the side of the trough and raised one knee under her hips to stop her sliding farther down. This time I wrapped my arms as tightly as I could around her, lower down, around her waist, under her ribs and I shoved her upward with all my might. My arms were shaking as her head and front legs cleared the top of the trough. But no matter how hard I pushed I wasn't strong enough to get the rest of her body out.

I needed Amy's help.

"Amy. Let's go." I said. "Let's go!"

Amy opened her eyes and saw what she needed to do. She dug her front toenails into the snow and pulled. I moved my hands under her and pushed. Together we moved her up an inch.

"Amy! Let's go!" I pleaded. She dug her toenails in and then her body went limp as though all the life had just gone out of her.

"Amy! Let's go!" I screamed. Her eyes flickered open and then closed. Using her last remaining strength, Amy dug her toenails in deep and pulled. I shoved as hard as possible and this time her body rose completely out of the trench.

Amy flopped over and lay motionless on the snow beside the creek. I climbed out and lay down beside my friend. After a couple of minutes Amy's eyes opened. With our noses almost touching, we stared deeply into each other's eyes, absorbing the joyous, wondrous fact that we were together again. It was the closest, most powerful moment I have ever shared with a dog.

Amy had stood in that nearly frozen water for somewhere close to twenty-four hours. While she rested I got up and looked around, trying to figure out what had happened. The answer was all right there in the snow. The creek under the railroad trestle had been covered by a thin layer of snow. For some reason Amy had walked over it and the snow caved in, dropping her into the icy water below. There were deep scratch marks on both sides of the trough where Amy had desperately tried to climb out.

The trough was narrow, so narrow, that if I had climbed off the road and up the snowbank in the usual place, the steep sides would have blocked my view and I would never have seen her. Why she didn't bark when I was searching close by, I will never know. Maybe she was too weak, too cold.

When Amy could walk, we headed back to my cabin. Just before we crested the hill, I gave Amy the hand signal to stop.

I walked forward and peered down into the dog yard. Every dog was sitting there staring up at me in silence. I smiled and they knew this time was different. As if on some invisible cue, they all stood up at the same time and looked past me.

With a flick of my wrist, Amy walked up and stood beside me. The instant she came into view, the entire dog lot went wild. They ran in circles, leaped high into the air, and barked wildly as if to say, *Amy's back! Amy's back!*

In that precious and glorious moment I saw love and happiness. Those dogs obviously had known something had happened to Amy and, as her friends, they had done everything they could to help for as long as it took.

I kneeled down beside Amy and gave her a hug. "How about those dogs? It's good to have friends you can count on. They love you, girl, and so do I."

After our long ordeal everyone was exhausted. Amy and I went into the cabin, the dogs curled up inside their houses, and we all took a very long and much needed nap.

2

DON'T JUMP OFF A CLIFF JUST BECAUSE SOMEONE TELLS YOU TO

As a sled dog, Jocko had a checkered career. He started life in a racing kennel, was booted off the team for being too slow, sold to another kennel, and booted off that team as well. When Jocko finally ended up in my kennel, he was a bit of a basket case—nervous and afraid to try anything for fear of failing. He had almost no confidence and would do nothing unless he was given a command. But, with patience and persistence we learned how to work together and trust one another. We formed a bond and became a team within a team.

In the same year Jocko joined my team as lead dog, we completed the Iditarod Trail Sled Dog Race 1,049 miles across Alaska from Anchorage to Nome. Now, three years later, here he was confidently leading us over a thousand miles across the barren arctic wilderness. Unlike the Iditarod, there was no trail on this journey. But I wasn't worried about getting lost. Over the years as lead dog Jocko had proven extraordinarily talented at figuring out where to go. And if he didn't know what to do, Jocko was smart enough to look to me for help. Between the two of us, we always got to where we wanted to go.

It was January 17, 1990, and the sun rose for the first time in fifty-four days. My eight-dog team and I were sledding across the north coast of Alaska heading for the village of Kaktovik, which was on Barter Island about ten miles away. We had traveled this route before and had come north again to spend time alone in the Arctic—the most pristine and beautiful place on earth—simply because we loved being here.

Around midday, for forty-two precious minutes the sun graced us with its pale light before once again sliding below the southern horizon. It gave no warmth and the temperature remained a frigid twenty-five degrees below zero. But I felt warm because, after blowing for three brutal days, the cold arctic wind had finally gone off to harass someone else. Other then the sound of our sled runners hissing over the snow, the land was silent.

Fortunately the long arctic twilight would last about three hours. So, I felt confident that we would reach the village before dark and decided to keep sledding instead of making camp.

During the first hour of travel after sunset we made almost four miles along the coast. To reach Barter Island we had to turn northeast and head out over the sea ice. Within a few minutes we came to chunks of ice the size of school desks scattered across the frozen sea. Jocko quickly sized up the situation, picked the best route, and led us around every obstacle. It was beautiful watching Jocko work and I loved how confident and relaxed he looked as he guided the team in the soft evening light.

But the farther offshore we traveled the worse it got, until we were moving among jagged slabs of ice as big as kitchen tables. Jocko struggled valiantly to lead us through the icy maze, but after more than an hour we had gone less than half a mile. Finally, the ice got so congested Jocko couldn't tell where to go anymore. But he was a thinking dog and he knew exactly what to do. He stopped. That was Jocko's way of telling me he needed help.

When Jocko stopped, the entire team stopped and waited for me to tell them what to do. That was how I trained them and they made me proud. These were not race dogs. Race dogs are usually trained to keep pulling no matter what. If one of them gets injured, that dog will be dropped at a checkpoint along the trail. My dogs were expedition dogs. They knew I would never ask them to pull a heavy sled over piled-up ice if that might get them hurt. In the Arctic there is almost never a place to get help for an injured dog. So my dogs waited.

Being taller than Jocko, I peered over the ice and saw a route. A soft call of "Gee," and Jocko veered to the right, leading us around a chunk of ice. "Haw," turned him left into a narrow, dark corridor. "All right," and he moved forward. Jocko followed my instructions, never stalling, always trusting that I was guiding him the right way.

Conditions continued to worsen. It was getting late and, when darkness fell, seeing a route through the maze became impossible even for me. The thermometer now read thirty-two degrees below zero. The penetrating cold made my fingers and toes ache, my nose and cheeks sting, and we were all tired and hungry. I was no longer sure where we were or how far it was to Kaktovik.

Jocko looked back at me as if to ask, *What now?*

I looked around us and thought, *We can't stop here. There's no place to camp.*

"I'll be right back."

I turned on my headlamp and followed its yellow beam into the icy chaos. The light only penetrated the darkness about fifty feet and it was difficult to figure out which way to go. Often what looked like a sure path dead-ended at a wall of ice with no way through, so I had to backtrack and seek a better way. On and on I went moving forward, turning back, heading left then right, and occasionally finding a route between the ice boulders that was wide enough for the sled to pass through. The ice was slick and in the shadowy maze I slipped and fell, painfully hitting my right knee against a sharp chunk of ice.

Careful! This is no time to get hurt.

There was something else to be concerned about. Along this coastal area is one of the densest concentrations of polar bears in the world. I knew they prowled constantly looking for something to eat. The farther I walked away from the team, the more nervous I got.

Keep your eyes open for bear tracks. Listen for the crunch of footsteps.

After more than a half an hour of scouting, I limped around a giant block of ice and came to an abrupt halt. Ahead of me was flat ice!

"Yahoo!!!" I yelled.

I turned around to go back to the dogs only to discover there was now a new problem. In wandering through the ice, I had created a maze of footsteps in the snow so confusing that I had absolutely no idea which ones led back to my team.

No problem. We had trained for this exact situation. I threw my head back and howled.

"Wooooo."

I knew I could count on my dogs to howl back. Sure enough, I heard "Woooooo."

I got my bearings and headed toward the dogs, only this

time, instead of walking normally, I shuffled along, dragging my feet. This created a little trail we could follow back to the flat ice. A few more sing-alongs and then over the breeze came the faint smell of corn chips. In the pure arctic air, untainted by other odors, that's what my team smells like.

By the time my nose led me all the way back to the team everyone was curled up with feet tucked under their bodies and noses buried under their tails.

"Okay, everybody up!" I called.

Nothing happened.

I clapped my hands and shouted, "Come on! Up, up! Everybody up!"

Nothing happened.

I knew the dogs wanted to stay where they were. But we couldn't, we had to move to the flat ice where there would be room to set up camp and get everyone fed.

Time for a little power lifting. I walked along the team and, one by one, I gently lifted each dog by their harness until their legs unfolded beneath them. When every dog was standing, I marched to the front of the team.

"That's the spirit!" I said in a cheery, singsong voice.

They stared at me bleary-eyed and swaying with fatigue. Clearly, no one was in the mood to go back to work.

Standing on my new trail, I looked at Jocko and said, "Okay, you just follow me. I'll be lead dog."

These were tough sled dogs and when I called, "All right!" Jocko gave a tug on the line and the dogs swung into action. About ten minutes later we reached the smooth ice. The dogs were so happy to be out of that nasty ice they surged forward moving past me at a fast trot.

Yikes! I made a flying leap and managed to grab the handlebar as the sled sped by and hopped onto the runners. *Phew! It would be pretty embarrassing if my team left me behind and made it to Kaktovik by themselves.* My bruised knee was throbbing and it was a relief to be able to ride again.

Minutes later the lights of Kaktovik popped up on the horizon. The dogs knew from experience that lights meant a village and a village meant rest. The dogs were energized and broke into a lope. I could feel their power surging through the sled. There was beauty in that moment. It was as though we were in a state of grace, as though the world was perfect and filled only with peace. The dogs, the sled, and I became as one and I knew they would not stop until we reached Kaktovik.

Soon I felt the sled angle up as the dogs pulled onto the low-lying island. It was very dark and I wasn't exactly sure where we were. But I knew from a previous visit that local people suggested visitors camp on Kaktovik Lagoon in front of the town. This was to protect visitors from polar bears that came to scavenge whale bones on the beach. The lagoon was protected from the beach by a well-traveled spit of land that served as a road and runway. So I was anxious to get down off the land and onto the lagoon where it would be safe to camp.

Feeling pretty certain the lagoon was to our left, I called softly, "Jocko, haw."

Jocko didn't move.

"Jocko, haw," I called a little louder. Again he didn't move.

"Jocko, haw!" I called sternly.

Jocko casually gazed off to his right as if to say, *I don't think so.*

What is the matter with this dog? Annoyed, I stomped up to the head of the team, grabbed Jocko by his harness, and pulled him to the left a few inches.

"I said, HAW!"

I ran back to the sled and gave it a shove.

Nothing!

Tired, cold, and now angry, I was in no mood for a mutiny! I stormed up to Jocko and yelled, "Look, don't you understand? We just have to go a little bit farther and we'll be down on the lagoon. THEN we stop."

When I pointed to the left, Jocko stared right, his glum face suggesting, *I really don't think so.*

"Okay. Fine! Nooo problem," I said sarcastically. "I'll be the lead dog again and stomp a little path again and then, if you're not too busy gazing off into the night, maybe you could **follow me!!!**"

With that, I flipped on my headlamp and took a step to the left. The yellow beam lit up a boulder-strewn beach about fifteen feet below.

"Ahhh!" I screamed, leaping backward. "Jocko! We're standing on the edge of a cliff!"

Jocko stared up at me as if to say, *I'm aware of that.*

Obviously we were not where I thought we were. By defying me, Jocko had saved us from plunging off the cliff and getting badly hurt or even killed. I knelt down beside Jocko, rubbed the back of his neck, and said, "I'm sorry for yelling at you."

I was horrified to realize something else; not only were we in the wrong place, I could see now that the beach was littered with whale bones! We were on the wrong side of the spit. This was the beach where polar bears came to scavenge! This was the most dangerous place in Kaktovik!

We needed to get away from there fast.

I climbed onto the sled runners for one last time that night and called, "Alright, Jocko." There was no need for me to say anything more. Jocko lead us away from the cliff, across the spit, and down to the safety of Kaktovik Lagoon, where I quickly set up camp.

After feeding the dogs, I snuggled down into my sleeping bag and let my mind wander over what had happened back there on the edge of the cliff. Somehow, in the darkness,

Jocko had known that to our left was nothing but air and danger. How he knew was a mystery. What I did know was that, in the years we had worked together, Jocko had gone from being a dog afraid of failing to being a dog with so much confidence and strength of character, he bravely refused to jump off a cliff just because someone told him to.

3

THE IDITAROD—
TEAMWORK BELOW ZERO

E very year on the first Saturday in March about 1,000 dogs show up in Anchorage, Alaska, to compete in a sled dog race. They run in teams of ten to sixteen dogs. Behind each team is a sled and on that sled stands a person called a musher. At 10:00 A.M. sharp, the announcer shouts, "Go!" and the race is on. Every two minutes a team starts down Fourth Avenue to the excited cheers of thousands of spectators. During the next two to three weeks these teams will wind through hundreds of miles of forest, and cross frozen rivers, mountains, and vast stretches of barren tundra. The goal of every musher is to drive their dog team over 1,000 miles to the gold-mining town of Nome. Getting lost and suffering from mind-numbing cold are their biggest fears.

This is the Iditarod Trail Sled Dog Race, the biggest single event in the state of Alaska and the longest sled dog race on earth.

In late 1981 I moved to Alaska and didn't even know the race existed. I spent my first year living at the Howling Dog Farm, home of world-famous Earl and Natalie Norris. In return for me feeding and cleaning up their large kennel, they gave me room and board, loaned me equipment and dogs, and taught me how to train and care for a team of sled dogs. During the 1982 race everyone at the farm stopped work every hour and gathered around the radio to hear the latest updates. Listening to the announcer tell stories about what was happening to mushers fired my imagination and I was hooked. By the end of the race I was determined that somehow I was going to compete in the 1983 Iditarod Race.

I knew from my first year of mushing that driving a dog team across a thousand miles of wilderness is a big goal and it was going to take a lot of work to get ready. I got a job working nights at a hospital as a registered respiratory therapist to support myself, moved out on my own, built a small cabin, bought some sled dogs, a sled and gear, and started my own dog team.

My dogs and I would be dependent on each other out in the wilderness. We needed to get fit and learn how to work together as a team. We started slowly, training one mile a day, then two then five. By watching each dog carefully I figured out which dogs worked best in what positions. The smartest and most obedient was Jocko so he became my lead dog. Every day we got stronger. By January my team was able to run over forty miles a day and we were working well together.

Our hard work paid off and on the first Saturday of March, 1983, I was standing on Fourth Avenue with my team. I could hardly believe this was actually happening. My dogs and I were going to run the Iditarod Trail Sled Dog Race! There were only eleven dogs in my team and we were going to compete against more experienced mushers with bigger teams and faster dogs. But that didn't matter. We were here, we were ready, and we were going to do our best.

At 11:26 A.M. the race announcer shouted, "Three! Two! One! Go!" As my team and I took off down Fourth Avenue the crowd cheered. Of course they cheered for every team but right then they were cheering for us. I smiled and waved at the people. It was very exciting and I felt like a rock star. Sixty-eight teams started out of Anchorage that day, ten women and fifty-eight men, each one riding a dream. But it was a long way to Nome and not every team would finish the race.

We passed through I don't know how many intersections where traffic stopped and waited for us to go by. Gliding past I waved at every vehicle.

Rock star!

Near the edge of town the trail cut through a snowbank

and went down into an icy, gravel-lined ditch where I was brought down to earth—literally. Just as we entered the cut, my left runner caught on something and the sled flipped over. My right hand raked across the gravel and my chin was smashed into the sled handle. The sled lurched to a stop.

"Are you okay?" asked a race volunteer.

"Ah . . . I'm fine," I said, weaving slightly.

Actually, I was so groggy from the blow to my chin I wasn't even sure where I was. After three or four seconds my thinking cleared up and I remembered I was in a sled dog race. When I looked at my team, they were standing patiently waiting for me to tell them what to do. *Thank goodness for all that training.*

"All right," I called and we continued down the trail. Within a few minutes my hand was hugely swollen and nearly useless and my chin was throbbing. I discovered later that a small bone in my right hand was cracked and the bottom of my chin had a one-inch gash. It was painful, but one thing was certain—I wasn't going to quit the race. So I became left-handed and kept going.

About two and a half hours later we came to the first checkpoint. I signed in and the checkpoint person counted my dogs and went through my sled to make sure I had the required gear—snowshoes, shovel, axe, sleeping bag, booties for the dogs, food for the dogs and me, and a package of ceremonial mail each musher carries to Nome. After the checker cleared me, the vet and I examined each dog to be sure they were in good shape. Everything was fine so off we went.

Over the next two days we went through seven checkpoints with no trouble. After Rainy Pass the trail took us across miles of nasty, windswept tundra and over a mountain pass. My hand was still badly swollen so I was driving one-handed. I was feeling pretty nervous as we approached the infamous Dalzell Gorge. This narrow, steep, twisting section of trail is the most frightening part of the race, and if we made it down the mountain in one piece, we still had to deal with the raging, icy cold Dalzell Creek. We would have to cross that creek on a snow bridge that may or may not be there.

Suddenly the trail narrowed and got really steep. *Here we go!*

A few inches to our right the mountain plunged straight down into the creek far below! *Fall off here and we might end up dead.* To make matters worse, the trail didn't go straight down; it twisted sharply left, right, left, right. If there's one thing sled dogs love, it's curves. On each one they sped up a little more and then a little more, going faster and faster.

Trying to control the sled was like riding a bucking bronco in a rodeo. Halfway down there were so many huge boulders crowding the trail, there was barely room for the sled to pass through. The dogs were rocketing downhill as we swerved around yet another sharp curve to the right. We were going too fast. We were out of control.

"Noooo!" I shouted. But it was too late. The sled struck a boulder with an ugly thud and was launched skyward.

We're going over the cliff!

Thankfully, in just the right spot, the trail turned sharply left and the sled was jerked out of midair by the dogs. Bam! The sled slammed back onto the trail. Several heart-stopping turns later, we arrived at the bottom of the gorge.

Whew!

The dogs finally slowed their pace a little and I relaxed for, oh, maybe five seconds. Then the bridge came into view.

Yikes!!

I couldn't believe my eyes! The so-called bridge was just four skinny logs and a thin covering of loose snow that stretched about ten feet across the raging creek.

We're supposed to cross on that thing???

Thankfully, from their low angle the dogs couldn't see how lousy the bridge was. I had a plan but it depended on my dogs trusting me. To get safely over the bridge we were going to have to work together as a team.

"All right! All right! All right!" I yelled (the command to run their tails off.) The dogs heard the tension in my voice and started running toward the bridge.

"All right! All right! All right!" By the time we reached the bridge, the team was running full out.

"All right! All right! Let's go!" The dogs raced onto the bridge. Their feet slipped on the slick logs. Snow started breaking away. The bridge was collapsing under us!

"All right!" Together the dogs gave it everything they had!

Then the welcome, raspy sound of runners on solid snow filled the air. We were across.

"We made it! Yahooo!" I yelled and waved at the imaginary cheering crowd. "Thank you, thank you. Thank you very much." *Rock star!*

I turned to look back over my shoulder at the collapsing bridge. I felt happy and proud that we'd made it and was just about to pat myself on the back when I looked forward again.

Crack!

The sled smashed into a tree! I was thrown off and tumbled onto the hard-packed snow. I got up and stared in disbelief at the damage. The handlebar—the only thing I have to hang on to that keeps me from falling off the sled—was broken into two pieces.

I was furious with myself. "How could you be so careless?" I yelled, accusingly.

I looked at my lead dog, Jocko, who was staring at me as if demanding to know, *Now what?*

"I have to fix this thing, that's what," I said in disgust.

I tied the team to the tree and they lay down for a nap. I found a branch about the size of the handlebar and taped it over the broken spot. It made a wobbly repair but it was good enough to keep going. About an hour later we arrived at the log cabin that serves as Rohn checkpoint. I asked if any planes were coming in with supplies. There were and I requested that they bring me a hockey stick to repair my handlebar. I could have ordered a new handlebar from the man who made my sled but he lived in New Hampshire and that would take too long. A sawed-off hockey stick clamped in place would work just fine.

Inside the cabin volunteers were serving mushers spaghetti, fruit cocktail, bread, hot chocolate, and coffee. For a few hours I sat beside a warm stove, talking with other mushers, swapping stories, and enjoying lots of laughs. Time spent at checkpoints is fun and I would have loved to stay longer. But the dogs don't get good rest because so many people are moving around and teams are coming and going. So once I repaired my sled, we took off just after seven in the evening.

By day five my dogs and I were very tightly bonded and we were working well together. They were showing amazing stamina and obeying my commands quickly. We had all learned to trust one another, and I was confident that if anything went wrong, the dogs would pull together and we would be okay. We had developed a strong team spirit and very soon that team spirit was going to pay off.

Our next challenge came when we hit a section of the trail known as The Burn. In 1978 thousands of acres of forest burned, leaving a landscape covered in fallen, charred trees. It is vast, open, and spectacular when seen from the ridges along the trail. I knew my dogs were not fast enough to be competitive and I wanted to enjoy this part of the journey so we stopped often. The openness had a relaxing effect on my dogs and they seemed to appreciate the peace of this barren land. Later, as the sun set and darkness started to fall over the land, the summit of Mount McKinley, the tallest mountain in North America, was stunning in its beauty as it caught the last rays of light, turning yellow, gold, pink, purple, and then disappearing into the blackness of night.

During the day I had become a little too relaxed and hadn't eaten enough food or drunk enough water. By evening I was hungry and thirsty and very cold. It was dark, about twenty below zero, and a steady north wind was blowing when we came to a fork in the trail around midnight. There was no sign showing us which way to go and both forks looked equally traveled. I don't know how long I stood there staring at that fork but after awhile I started to realize something was wrong. I couldn't make a simple decision whether to go left or right and I was so cold my body was shaking.

Your body temperature is too low. You're getting hypothermic. Stop and take care of yourself.

My injured hand was so cold it was almost useless and I was afraid it might get frostbitten. If that happened I would have to quit the race. I desperately needed to find shelter from the wind and get warmed up. But there was nothing around for miles so I was going to have to be creative and use what I had with me.

Jocko had developed into an extraordinary leader and, when I told him to leave the trail, he led the team right up into the middle of the fork without hesitation. Now we could camp without blocking the trail in case someone else came along.

We stopped and I called, "Jocko, come haw."

This is an uncommon and difficult command that requires the lead dog to make a sharp left and walk back in the opposite direction of the sled. Jocko looked back at me and I could see the puzzled look in his eyes as though he was thinking, *Why are we doing this? Something's wrong.* Though he didn't understand what we were doing, Jocko turned and started walking back toward the sled. As he did this the other dogs turned and followed along behind him until everyone was walking toward me. When Jocko had brought the entire team alongside the sled, I called, "Whoa. Everyone take a break." All the dogs lay down at once.

My good hand was stinging from the cold and I was so exhausted it took nearly all my strength to drag my sleeping bag out. I was shaking from the cold as I wedged down between the dogs and sled and struggled into the sleeping bag. Finally, I had shelter from the wind.

The dogs were practically piled on top of one another and I could feel the heat radiating from their bodies. When I handed out snacks, everyone politely waited their turn. No one growled and no one tried to steal anyone's food. My mind still felt foggy but, as I drank hot tea from my thermos, warmth slowly spread through my body and my thinking started to clear up. I smiled and reached out to softly touch each dog's head. Lying beside this big pile of warm fur that was my dog team, I was grateful for all they had given me.

Jocko was right beside me and I stroked his face. "Look at us all snuggled together helping each other out. We've got ourselves quite a team."

As it turned out the right fork of the trail was the *right* fork. The rest of our journey to Nome was full of fun and we were happy sledding over those miles. A few days later, after more than twenty days on the trail, my team and I reached the outskirts of Nome. Within minutes, I could see the big burled arch that marks the end of the trail! We were actually going to finish the Iditarod Trail Sled Dog Race!

When we crossed the finish line, we were team number fifty-one out of fifty-four to finish the race that year. It was just past midnight, but, amazingly, the street was lined with people cheering for my dogs and me as though we had won first place.

I smiled and waved. *Rock star!*

After feeding my dogs and watching them drift off to sleep, I thought about all we had been through during the race. I felt proud and happy. We had overcome many challenges through teamwork and that's what the Iditarod is all about.

4

THE BULLY

When I was six years old there was a bully in my class. I was the youngest and by far the smallest kid in my class and, almost every day after school as I walked home alone, this bully would run up behind me, grab my arm, and punch me three times in the stomach. My mother called the school but they did nothing. She called the bully's parents but they also did nothing. In the end it was up to me to look out for myself and I had no idea what to do. I wish I had known my dog Amy back then. I like to think that I would have been brave enough to try her solution.

More than forty years later, on a warm, sunny afternoon, my dog Amy and her best friend Chinook strolled along a gravel road, stopping occasionally to sniff in the sparse roadside grass. It was their favorite place to walk because it was quiet and few cars passed by.

Chinook was an enthusiastic, happy-go-lucky thirteen-year-old dog with a soft, brown coat. She looked something like a Chesapeake Bay retriever but had long ears that stood straight up and tipped over on the ends, giving her an everlasting look of surprise. Amy was eleven, tan, husky-looking, and about the same size as Chinook. She was even tempered and moved with quiet confidence.

About half a mile down the road, there was a big gray house with a huge yard surrounded by a tall, chain-link fence. Amy and Chinook had never paid any attention to the gray house until the day the new dog moved in.

The new dog was big and their first encounter with him was pretty rude. As Chinook and Amy walked the road near his house, the new dog ran up to the fence, snarling and barking. Amy stopped, walked up to the fence opposite him, and casually sniffed the ground in front of her. Then, as if to say, *I'm not impressed,* Amy walked away like he didn't exist. The new dog grew silent as he watched her leave.

Always eager to make a new friend, Chinook pranced over to the fence, wagged her tail, and pulled her lips back in a big doggie smile.

The new dog flew into a rage. "Arrrggghhh!!" he snarled.

He grabbed the fence with his teeth, tugging and shaking it as if he thought he could tear the fence apart. Like most bullies he had too much self-confidence and expected Chinook to cower in front of him. But instead, Chinook cocked her head sideways as if to ask, *I suppose this means you don't want to play with me?* Never one to let anything get her down, Chinook happily ran off to catch up with Amy.

Every time Amy and Chinook walked by, the new dog behaved the same way. If Chinook even glanced at him, he would launch into a frenzy of vicious barking and bite the fence.

The fence that surrounded the yard was about five feet high and had a gate that was always closed. With each passing day the new dog seemed more and more determined to get out of his yard. He began standing on his back legs and banging his front paws against the fence. Then he'd drop down and furiously dig, trying to tunnel under the fence.

One evening as Amy and Chinook neared the fence they could see the bully dog lying on the grass near the house, so they moved to the opposite side of the road. They were almost past when he raised his head and spotted them. He jumped to his feet, locked his eyes on Chinook, and charged across the yard, going faster and faster. Just as he reached the fence, he made a mighty leap and hurled himself upward.

He soared in a high graceful arc, rising higher and higher. Chinook watched in wide-eyed amazement as though she were thinking, *Wow! A flying dog!*

His front legs cleared the top but his body slammed into

the fence. He fell back to earth and landed with a dull thud. The impact knocked the wind right out of him.

As he lay on the ground gasping for breath, Amy walked over and looked through the fence at him as though she were thinking, *Nope, still not impressed.*

Then Chinook and Amy turned and quietly walked away.

Months passed with no change in the bully's behavior. About the time Chinook turned fourteen and Amy turned twelve, the difference in their ages began to show. Amy still walked like a healthy young dog, but Chinook was becoming a little unsteady on her feet.

Then one day something happened that changed their walk along the road forever. It was a lovely sunny day, perfect for an afternoon stroll. The bully was lying in the middle of the yard, gnawing on a huge bone. When he saw Amy and Chinook approaching, the bully slowly rose to his feet, spit out his bone, and fixed his eyes on Chinook. With lightning speed, he charged straight across the yard.

Only this time the front gate was wide open and he ran right through it!

Amy's eyes flared with fear. Chinook looked at the ground, not knowing what to do.

The bully curled his lips back as he ran full out. He opened his mouth wide. He was almost on Chinook. He was going to sink his teeth into her neck! He was going to kill her!

In that moment, in one single step, Amy placed herself between the bully and Chinook.

The bully skidded to a halt—teeth bared, jaws snapping, throat growling—just inches from Amy's face.

Amy didn't even blink.

The bully curled back his lips, showing his sharp front teeth.

Amy did not back down. She stood perfectly still and stared straight into the bully's eyes. When he moved over one step to the right, Amy moved to block him. He snapped and snarled as though he was going to tear her apart. Amy simply raised her head a little higher and stared back in silence.

Amy had made a decision. No matter where he moved, no matter how ferociously he growled, she was not going to let the bully get to her friend.

The attack lasted less than a minute and then the bully grew quiet. He turned his head and looked down the empty road as though confused about what to do next. After a few more seconds he lowered his head, turned around, and walked home in silence. Then, Amy walked over to where Chinook stood waiting. Side by side, they quietly finished their walk.

Thinking back on that terrible day, I realize that Amy must have been as frightened as Chinook. When the bully charged, Amy had choices. She could have stood back and done nothing, leaving Chinook helpless to defend herself. She could have charged the bully and gotten into a terrible fight. But she didn't do either of those things. Instead, Amy confronted the bully in silence, showed no aggression, and simply refused to back down. And it worked perfectly.

Whatever happened to the bully? For the next few days he only watched in silence as Amy and Chinook passed by. Then one day he was gone, never to be seen again.

5

HE WAS BORN THAT WAY

This story is about a sled dog named Roald. He saw things differently from most other dogs and lived life his own way. Roald was a hardworking team dog but perhaps his greatest contribution was to teach his sisters and me to accept others, even if they are a little different.

On a cold winter's night three tiny sled dog puppies were born in a snug doghouse lined with straw. Outside, big fluffy snowflakes fell softly to the ground creating a huge white quilt across the land. It was a beautiful beginning for puppies destined to spend their entire lives out-of-doors.

Roald was the only male and he had a white coat with big gray patches all over. His two sisters were named Sojo and Anna.

Like all puppies, they were born deaf and blind but had an excellent sense of smell. As soon as they were born, Anna and Sojo snuggled up to their mother and fell asleep. But Roald lay shivering in the straw barely ten inches from his mother, frantically sniffing the air with his tiny nose. He seemed to have no idea what to do.

His mother tried nudging him toward her with her nose. But instead of moving closer Roald let out a sharp screech and pulled away. His mother looked up at me with questioning eyes, as if she were saying, *I don't know what to do. Can you help him?*

I picked Roald up as gently as possible. His tiny legs flailed in the air. When I placed him beside his mother's tummy, Roald whimpered as though he was frightened and confused.

I cupped his mother's face in my hand and said, "It'll be okay. He'll be fine." After a couple more restless minutes, Roald fell into an uneasy asleep.

During the next few days, I noticed that any change in Roald's world upset him. If Sojo or Anna shifted even a little, Roald would launch himself into a whining panic. If his mother tried to sooth him with the soft touch of her tongue, he trembled as though terrified. If I stroked him gently with one finger, he screeched and shrank away. Roald whimpered almost constantly and nothing brought him comfort.

At about two weeks old, the puppies' eyes and ears opened, bringing sight and sound into their world. When the puppies heard the sound of my footsteps crunching on the snow, Anna and Sojo quickly waddled to the door of their house. They were always excited to see me. But Roald was different. He hung back and if I tried to pet him he would screech and tuck himself into the farthest corner of the doghouse. It was heartbreaking to see him sitting in there looking so frightened.

I had never known a puppy that acted like Roald and I had no idea what was wrong. Everyone who visited my kennel had a theory.

"Maybe he's just shy."

"Maybe it's a stage and he'll outgrow it."

"Maybe he's autistic."

I didn't know the answer. The only thing I knew for certain was that while I waited nothing magic happened. So I decided to play it by ear and work with him a little bit every day. I was determined that together we would find the key to understanding his personality and that key would give Roald the best chance at becoming a happy dog.

Our work began the next morning. My plan was to spend about fifteen minutes every day sitting beside his doghouse doing nothing, so he could get used to having me near him. That first morning I sat in a lawn chair, but the chair terrified him so I put it away and sat on the ground. I sat next to his doghouse every day for a week, but for the entire time I sat there, Roald stayed inside his house or hid behind his mother.

One day when Roald was about six weeks old, I was sitting on the steps in the sunshine, relaxing. I noticed Roald straining to get a little stick out from under his house, but it was just beyond the reach of his paw. He stood up and stared off into space with a thoughtful look on his face. Then he lowered his head back to the ground and looked at the stick. He moved to the next side of his doghouse and the next, until he had seen the stick from all four sides. Then, without hesitation, Roald walked around to the back of the doghouse where the stick lay closest to him. He crouched down, stretched his little front leg under the house, snagged the stick with his claws, and dragged it out.

Thrilled by his success, Roald had his own private celebration. He grabbed the stick with his teeth and flung it into the air. When the stick landed on the ground, he snatched it up and raced in cirlces around his house.

What a wonderful moment that was! This was the first time I had ever seen my little guy happy. And I finally understood a couple of things about Roald. He was smart and he was a loner who was perfectly happy playing by himself.

Figuring things out was also something Roald obviously enjoyed and was good at. So, I began a new campaign, one that would help him figure out on his own how to trust me. The day after his stick triumph I sat down beside the doghouse once again. Roald cautiously sniffed the ground around me. Casually, I extended my right arm and lay my hand on the ground, open and palm up. When Roald approached me from the right, I looked slightly to my left so he would think I wasn't watching him. He quickly sniffed my fingertips, then turned around and walked back to chew on his latest stick.

The next day I sat down and extended my open hand. "Hey, Roald," I said softly, "How about a little action?"

When he approached my hand, I wiggled one finger. He jumped back and said, "Woof!"

I wiggled my finger again, but this time he didn't bark, he just stared at it. On the fifth day we had a breakthrough. Roald allowed me to scratch him under his chin very lightly with that one finger. Within a few days he was letting me stroke his back. But, like a cat, when he had enough touching, Roald would get up and walk away. But, every day, no matter how gently I stroked him, the first touch of the day always made him flinch.

After a couple of weeks, Roald finally started to trust me and our time spent together was happier and more relaxed. But he still had social issues with his sisters. From my cabin window I saw him watching Sojo and Anna playing. He'd step forward as though he wanted to join them but then he'd back off. When Roald finally tried to join in, the girls played with him for a minute or two but then they went back to playing with each other. It was as though Roald didn't understand how to play with his sisters and they didn't understand how to play with him.

Another issue for Roald was that he would not leave the dog lot to join his sisters and me for our walks. But Roald needed to have broader experiences to help him grow, so I decided we would go for our own walks, just the two of us. By now I knew I had to take things slowly with Roald, so I strolled over to his house and, without making eye contact, said, "Come on, Roald. Let's go for a walk." Then, I turned and leisurely walked away. To my great surprise and delight Roald followed me and walked right through the invisible barrier that had so long stopped him from leaving the dog lot!

Don't mess this up. Leave him alone and let him do whatever he wants.

We stopped every few inches as Roald sniffed nearly every blade of grass and twig. He wasn't much interested in the walking part, he just wanted to check things out. Best of all, I realized he now felt comfortable enough with me to go beyond his former limits. During that fifteen-minute walk, we went all of ten feet—but it was a start.

By the time Roald was a year old he had gained considerable confidence and we often walked three or four miles together. But he still had serious social problems with his sisters. As adults each dog was now attached to their doghouse on a ten-foot length of chain. When I unsnapped Sojo and Anna's chains and we left for our walks, Roald would jump on top of his doghouse, turn his back to us, and stare off into the forest. With his chin held high, he looked as though he were saying *I'm not the least bit interested in going for a walk.* But when he peeked over his shoulder at us, his sad eyes showed it hurt him to be left behind.

Unbeknown to me, things were churning in that brilliant brain of his. Roald had been out there on walks, he knew they were fun, he wanted to be included, and he had a plan.

One morning Roald did something that shocked us all. Just as the girls and I got to the road at the start of our walk, Roald jumped off his doghouse and began lunging and lunging at the end of his chain. Normally chains don't break but that day a link in Roald's chain snapped in half and he was suddenly free.

And then that dog ran. He didn't run away from us, he ran full speed toward us! We stood watching bug-eyed as he raced past us, spun around, and raced past us again and again. It was as though he was smashing through an invisible barrier. Smashing it to pieces, and discovering what it felt like to be free.

He finally stopped right in front of me, ribs heaving, eyes fixed firmly on the ground by my feet. It was his way of saying, *I want to come along, too.*

I wanted to kneel down and hug him. But Roald hated being hugged, so instead I just said in a calm voice, "Hey, Roald. Looks like you're ready to go for a walk." His tail gave a tiny swish. The girls were excited and tried to play with him, but he just ignored them and set off down the road at a brisk pace.

"Well, girls, we better get going before he gets too far ahead." And off we went, together at last.

It was a momentous day. Somehow, Roald had found the courage to run toward what he feared instead of away from it.

When he was old enough, Roald joined my dog team and became an excellent sled dog. He was never a team leader but Roald's willingness to work hard made him a very valuable member of my team. Roald never stopped worrying about

new situations and he remained a loner for his entire life. But that was just fine with him, and with us.

We all learned a lot from Roald being in our lives. In his brilliant brain, he figured out how to be himself and still fit in to his society. Roald's sisters and I eventually came to understand that he had no desire to be among us, just near us. For Roald that was enough. All we had to do was accept Roald as he was and let him live life in his own unique way. It was a powerful lesson because that is what we all want: the gift of acceptance.

6

WHATEVER IT TAKES

A lot of miles had passed under my runners since we had completed the Iditarod Race. One by one my dogs had retired and I had an entirely new team. A dog named Douggie was my new leader and my team and I were going to try to cross the Arctic on a 2,500-mile solo expedition. It was the biggest, most difficult challenge we had ever taken on.

Douggie was a big, seventy-five pound, hardworking bundle of energy and muscle. He looked vaguely like a St. Bernard with a blocky head and flop ears and he was black except for some white on his muzzle, a splash of white on his chest, and white ankles with black spots. He was a happy dog that loved to play when he wasn't wearing his harness. Douggie became number one lead dog because he followed my commands very well, had the confidence to stay out in front of the team, and always managed to lead the team through every challenge.

As I packed my sleds with gear and supplies I thought about just how different this journey was compared to the Iditarod Trail Sled Dog Race. The Iditarod was just over 1,000 miles and the year we did it, the trail passed through twenty-four villages and rest stops. The longest distance between any two villages was ninety miles. Not only was this journey across the Arctic two-and-a-half times as long, we would stop at only nine villages, because that's all there are along our entire route. The longest distance between villages was over 360 miles. The Iditarod took fewer than three weeks to complete. This expedition, because of the harsh terrain and severe weather, would require several months.

On Valentine's Day my team and I were in Barrow, Alaska, the northernmost city in the United States. This was our big day and we were ready to start our long journey. By two o'clock a predicted storm had failed to arrive and the sky was still clear blue. If we left now, we could still get in some miles, so I decided to take off.

As I climbed onto the lead sled, I felt a little nervous because we had to sled through a crowded neighborhood to get out of town and there was no trail.

"All right!" I called. *Make me proud, Douggie.*

And he did! My pride and joy, number one lead dog Douggie, led us across a yard, past a snowmobile, between two houses, around a neighbor's garage, down a driveway, across a road, across a field, around a telephone pole, and out onto the tundra as though he did this every day.

"Whew!" I whispered to myself.

As we moved away from Barrow, I had only happy, positive thoughts. There were my dogs in front of me, all eight of them, doing what they do best—dragging me across the snow on a sled. This was really happening! My dream was becoming reality.

There were four females and four males in my team—Douggie, Anna, Alice, Matt, Roald, Sojo, Lucy, and Robert. All the dogs were related in one way or another and had known each other their entire lives. They were good, honest dogs, with thick hair to protect them from the cold. Every one of them was extremely hardworking and walked on feet toughened by many months and miles of training. These dogs were not fast, but their other strengths made them well-suited for a long journey across the Arctic.

To make up for our late start, we traveled until it got dark and made twenty-eight miles the first day. After the dogs had eaten and were snuggled beside one another, I sat down next to Douggie.

"Everyone thinks we're going to fail. They say we shouldn't do this, much less do it alone, because it's too dangerous. Fred says you dogs are nothing but a bunch of clunkers." I glanced over at Anna. "Dave says Anna is too small and shouldn't even be in the team. They say you don't have enough experience to be a lead dog."

"Well, the one thing *I* know about us is that we have guts. We're willing to work hard and *I* believe in us."

I got up on my knees and looked straight into Douggie's eyes. "Always remember, you're no clunker. You're a lead dog. This team respects you and you're going to lead us right across this continent."

I leaned forward and gave Douggie a smooch on his nose. He flicked his tail and then, in a flash, slurped his big, wet tongue across my face.

"Oh, you!" I said laughing. Douggie pulled his lips back in a doggie smile and thumped his tail on the snow.

Burrowed into my sleeping bag I thought about what we were taking on. I had no sponsors so I had to borrow every penny I could get my hands on. That meant buying only what we needed. There were no luxuries and my only entertainment was one small, paperback book. Unlike races, there would be no planes flying over to check on us. No one would be offering me hot coffee and spaghetti in a cozy cabin in the forest, because there were no cabins and no forest. No one would keep a hole open in the ice for us to get water. I would have to melt snow any time we needed water. If my sled broke, no one would fly in a repair part. And the scariest of all, if we fell through the ice, no one would come along to pluck us out.

But the greatest difference was the trail. The entire Iditarod Trail is marked with tripods, sticks stuck in the snow, and signs on trees. On this journey, there would be no trail at all. We would have to find our way along the entire 2,500 miles of arctic wilderness. If we succeeded, this would be the longest solo dogsled journey by a woman in recorded history.

Right from the start the weather slowed us down. We sat out a nasty one-day storm and I spent half the next day digging out. By the sixth day, we were getting low on food but I wasn't worried because I knew we were close to the first cache. The cache contained food for me and the dogs and stove fuel. During the two months before the expedition we had trained by sledding across the north coast of Alaska putting out food caches along the first three hundred miles of our route. That meant we wouldn't have to carry so much weight on the sleds in the beginning of the trip. These caches were all placed out in the open on the snow and I knew, in the time-honored tradition of wilderness travel, no one would steal anything from them.

As we sledded east, a dense mist made it difficult to see very far ahead. What I could see looked hillier than I remembered, and after awhile, I was sure we were too far south. If we didn't change course, we would miss the cache. If we missed the cache we wouldn't have enough food to get us to the next one.

"Haw, Douggie, haw," I called. This is the command to go left, which would get him moving toward the cache again.

He swung left but then quickly swung back and kept going in the wrong direction.

"Douggie, haw," I called again. But again he swung left and then back in the wrong direction. He did this over and over and over. Douggie was determined to keep going his way and I was determined to go my way.

Douggie's stubbornness was making me angry. He acted as though he didn't even notice that I was now screaming my head off.

"Douglas! If we miss this cache, we're going to eat *you* for dinner!"

But did he listen? Nope. He just kept merrily leading our team in the wrong direction.

Just then we crested a hill and there, about a hundred yards straight ahead, was our cache.

I could hardly believe it. *How did you do that, Douggie?* With no trail and through thick mist, he had led us across miles of wilderness and somehow managed to bring us to the cache. What was more baffling, and a little embarrassing, was that he had done all of this in spite of me!

When we pulled up to the cache, I got off the sled and walked up to Douggie.

"Okay, I admit it. You were right. I was wrong. I'm sorry for yelling at you."

As though he understood that I was embarrassed, Douggie barked a playful, **"Woof!"**

Then Anna barked and soon all the dogs were barking and bouncing up and down. They threw their heads back and howled with joy. In my world, there is nothing more fun than a group howl with your dog team, so I threw my head back and joined in.

"Wooooo! Wooooooooo!"

We had found the cache. All was forgiven and we were a team again.

Weeks later, on March 10 we reached the border between the United States and Canada. No customs here. The only thing that marked the border was a three-foot-high, wooden obelisk reading "U.S." on one side and "Canada" on the other. After a quick picture, we sledded over the imaginary line into Canada. We were also traveling along another imaginary line, one biologists had drawn on the maps of this area showing the southern range of polar bears and the northern range of grizzly bears. It was a dangerous place to be sledding, that's for sure.

More storms slowed us down, but on March 17, nearly 700 miles into our journey, we finally reached the Mackenzie River delta. This mighty river flows north over 1,000 miles and empties into the shallow Beaufort Sea. The entire delta is covered in a very dense thicket of willows about two to four feet high that was impossible to sled through. From my map I could see there were several channels through the delta and they were all connected to one another in a giant maze. Since the channels were frozen this time of year, they would make a wonderful zigzag trail all the way across the delta.

Anna, who was still very young, had been showing promise as a lead dog, so I moved her up beside Douggie to get in some practice. As we sledded along a channel, I was confident that this was going to be an easy crossing.

But just a few minutes later a huge brown grizzly bear lumbered out of the thicket about a hundred yards ahead of us. It started crossing the channel and didn't seem to notice us. But the dogs certainly noticed it!

None of these dogs had ever seen a bear before. They had no idea what to do. Anna dropped her head and led the charge. In a flash we were rocketing straight toward the bear.

I smashed the brake into the snow and screamed, "Whoa! Whoa!" Douggie kept trying to help slow the team down but the dogs were too excited and kept running.

"Whoa!" I yelled, again. "Whoa!" Douggie looked back at me as if to say, *I'm trying. I'm trying.* But he had to keep running or get run over by the team.

"Whoa!" I screamed.

We were getting closer and closer to the bear.

The bear turned its head as it walked and looked at us.

We were now 100 feet from the bear.

Then, in a flash of genius, Douggie turned sharply left and led the entire team right into the willows and got us stuck.

As Douggie stood gasping for breath, he looked back at me as if to say, *I did it. I got them stopped.*

Why the bear didn't turn on us, I will never know. Maybe it thought we were a pack of wolves or maybe it was hunting something. All I know is that it disappeared into the thicket and we never saw it again.

In one of the stormiest arctic winters on record, we endured one blizzard after another. Nevertheless, by April 21 we had managed to travel over 1,200 miles, reaching the half-way point of our journey.

"Big day today, puppy dogs. We're halfway through," I said cheerily. "Time to celebrate!" I reached into my sled bag and brought out eight steaks, which I had been hoarding for this very special day. Every dog got a big, thick steak and every dog devoured theirs in about ten seconds.

Between storms the spring weather felt practically hot to us, with temperatures often rising above zero. It was hardest on Douggie with his thick, black coat and he was beginning to look tired. Before we left the tiny village of Bay Chimo, Native people told us that it would get cold again and there would be enough ice to travel on. But I was worried because a lot of snow and ice had melted and we still had to cross Queen Maud Gulf. It was roughly 200 miles across and famous for thin and shifting ice. This would be one of the most difficult challenges of our entire journey.

On May 10 I set up camp beside a giant boulder at the bottom of a hill near a place known as Half Way Point. The next morning, after loading up the sleds, I put Douggie's harness on him. Just as I was leading him to the front of the gang-line, two caribou stepped out from behind the boulder. Douggie leaped forward, jerking his collar out of my hand.

"Douggie," I called, "Come."

No response. The caribou looked at Douggie and then trotted off with their noses in the air as though they were challenging him to chase them.

"Douggie," I called again, "Come here!"

Douggie looked back at me and I could see it in his eyes: storms, a grizzly bear, and now the taunting caribou. It was all too much. No more Mr. Responsibility. Douggie had had enough of hard work and today he was going to have some fun!

And just like that, Douggie took off after the caribou. I couldn't believe it.

I harnessed the other dogs in record time and we went after our runaway leader. The caribou turned right and headed toward a hill with Douggie closing the gap. The dogs and I made a sharp right turn. If we were fast enough, we could catch Douggie before he reached the hill. But we were too slow. Douggie ran by just a few feet in front of us looking quite happy with himself and charged up the hill after the caribou. The hill was steep, strewn with boulders, and had almost no snow. There was no way we could follow.

Douggie was gone.

I set up camp by the same giant boulder and we waited. As the hours passed and Douggie didn't return, I began to worry that he might have gotten lost. For three days Anna led as we sledded around the area, searching and calling his name, always returning to the same camp, but we found no sign of Douggie. I was beside myself with worry and fear. There were wolves in these hills and if they found Douggie, he would have no chance against them.

We sledded to the community of Cambridge Bay where I asked for help. I left the dogs in town while two men and I returned to Half Way Point and searched on snowmobiles. We found nothing. We traveled deep into the hills looking for some sign. Nothing. I even stood on a mountaintop and shouted, "Douggie come! Douggie, come!" There was no response, not even an echo.

By then Douggie had been missing for six days. That night, back in Cambridge Bay I dreamed Douggie was killed by a pack of wolves. My dream was so vivid, I was sure it was real.

I was brokenhearted and wanted to quit the expedition, but everyone I talked to encouraged me not to give up when we had come so far. Without Douggie's strength and leadership, I wasn't sure we could do it. But I decided we had to try.

The next morning, just as we were preparing to leave, some people from Bay Chimo, the last village we had visited, pulled into town on a snowmobile. They smiled and one of them said, "We saw your dog over by Half Way Point."

I could hardly believe my ears! Douggie was alive! I thanked the man and jumped on my sled. With hopes riding high we sped away. The dogs picked up on my excitement and we covered seventy-two miles in twenty-four hours. When we reached Half Way Point, I got off my sled and turned slowly in a circle searching for Douggie. The land was empty.

"Douggie!" I called.

Silence.

"Douggie, where are you!"

We searched all day but found nothing. I knew that if we left Half Way Point without Douggie, we would be leaving him behind forever.

No! Douggie had always come through for us and we were not going to abandon him. This time we would keep searching until we found him.

The next day we got a break. A group of snowmobilers came by and set up camp. They had a radiophone and let me use it. I broadcast to everyone in the area, "I will pay $500 to anyone who finds my dog Douggie and returns him to me."

Immediately, a man responded with a question, "Does that mean dead or alive?"

The question shocked and frightened me. Had someone already shot Douggie?"

"Douggie must be returned to me at Half Way Point alive and unharmed," I replied firmly.

The next day another snowmobiler came by and told me that Douggie was back in the village of Bay Chimo, 135 miles away! The man said a family would bring him to me the next day. But the next day came and went and no one showed up.

The following morning, I could stand it no longer. "Come on everybody, we're going to Bay Chimo."

We headed south and after about an hour I saw a dark speck in the distance. As it drew closer, I could see it was a snowmobile. When it was even closer, I could see the snowmobile was pulling a trailer sled with a big box on it and there was something dark inside the box.

Please, please, please let that be Douggie.

We stopped and waited. When the man driving the snowmobile pulled up, he was smiling. Behind him his wife and daughter were smiling. In the box on the trailer sled sat Douggie! He was alive!

I ran over and threw my arms around Douggie, but he didn't even recognize me. He just sat there staring into the bottom of the box with dull eyes, his face a complete blank. Douggie's ordeal had been too much for him and he was in a state of shock. Seeing him like that was heartbreaking. I bent over and gently kissed the top of his head.

Douggie's rescuers, Henry, Lena, and their daughter, Karen, helped me lift him from the box and I led him slowly over to his teammates. Just like before, he just stood there looking blank, as though he had never seen the dogs before.

I knew the team was excited to see Douggie and I expected they would bark and mob him. But they didn't. Douggie needed patience, tenderness, and compassion and they gave him all those things. The entire team slowly and silently gathered around him. Ever so softly, they sniffed him all over, as though he were made of something fragile, something that could break if not handled with care. Even their tails swished gently.

Then, as if coming out of a fog, Douggie's face began to change. A look of recognition slowly spread over his face. When Douggie began wagging his tail, I knew he would be okay.

It was the most compassionate moment I have ever witnessed among my dogs.

And then there was more.

Douggie was thin and needed time to rest and recuperate. Happily he still had an appetite and ate four small meals in twelve hours. That evening, Douggie happened to be standing next to Lucy as I put down their bowls. Douggie was ravenous and devoured his meal in seconds. Then he nudged Lucy over and started gulping her food.

Lucy was not a dog to let something like that go and I expected her to shove him back. But she didn't, she just backed off. Calmly she sat down, turned her head away, and pretended not to notice Douggie stealing her dinner. Clearly, Lucy understood Douggie needed the food more than she did and she was willing to go hungry so Douggie could have more to eat. (Of course, I didn't let Lucy go hungry. I fixed her another bowl of food.)

As I watched this last little drama unfold, I smiled and my eyes filled up with tears. I wished I could tell my dogs how much I appreciated what they did for Douggie on this beautiful day. No matter what had happened on our journey, Douggie had always come through for his team. Now, when he needed them most, Douggie's teammates had come through for him. That evening our camp was filled with light and love and the joy of being together again.

7

HEROES ONE AND ALL

Douggie was back! But I knew we weren't out of the woods yet. Douggie was a tough dog but he was so thin and weak after being lost, I knew he wouldn't be able to work until he got his strength back.

While he was recovering, I decided to move Anna to number one lead dog. She had done amazingly well leading the team during the search for Douggie, but the switch worried me some. During training, people told me that fourteen-month-old Anna was too young and too small for such a long journey. And we still had 800 difficult miles to go. Being lead dog, making decisions, and following commands all day puts a huge amount of responsibility on a dog. I wondered if Anna, so young and inexperienced, could hold up under the pressure.

But Anna had worked hard and earned a place on the team. Over the past months she had worked her way from team dog to number two leader, just behind Douggie. And like all true leaders, Anna did more than just stay out in front. She had willingly shouldered her new responsibilities and worked tirelessly. When we couldn't find Douggie and I was sick with worry, Anna's positive attitude inspired me.

As we waited for Douggie to get stronger, I worried about something else. Temperatures were continuing to rise to alarming levels, often getting above freezing. If it kept up there wouldn't be enough ice left for us to cross Queen Maud Gulf and we wouldn't be able to finish our journey.

After two days of eating and resting, I kneeled beside Douggie and asked, "How are you feeling? Are you ready to get back in the harness?"

Douggie flicked his tail and slurped his tongue across my glasses, nearly knocking me over. I took that as a yes. "Okay, I guess we'll give it a try."

I knew Douggie was still too weak to do much pulling, but it would be enough if he could just walk fast enough to keep up. I put Douggie beside Anna, hoping his presence would help her stay confident. We set out at a slow pace and took a lot of short breaks. I was relieved to see that he could keep up.

It was a good thing, too, as we were nearing the most difficult part of our journey. Soon we would have to cross Queen Maud Gulf, a stretch of thin, broken, shifting ice more than 260 miles across. Not since Santa asked Rudolph to guide his sleigh on that foggy night has one four-legged critter been asked to do so much.

This would be Anna's greatest challenge yet.

We headed out onto the ice on May 28. Each day the temperature grew warmer: Thirty-four . . . forty-two . . . forty-eight . . . And on June 1 it reached a shocking sixty-eight degrees. Douggie, with his thick, black coat, was suffering from the heat and barely able to keep up. The other dogs were still working but they too were overheating and slowing down. To help make things easier for them, I walked behind the sled and pushed.

We were now sledding through three to six inches of slush atop ever-softening ice. Most of the time we were engulfed by thick fog and had to carefully avoid giant holes in the ice. Sometimes the thin ice broke under us and a dog would plunge into the icy sea. One day four dogs fell in at once. It took all my strength to pull them out one by one and, for the rest of that day, we were all so terrified sometimes even Anna didn't want to go forward.

Whenever she stopped I called, "All right, Anna. Let's go." Being the leader that she was, Anne would summon her courage, lean into her harness, and start moving forward again.

I changed our schedule so we traveled only at night when it was coolest. But it was still terribly hard pulling for the dogs and Douggie was staggering.

On June 5, Douggie's tenth birthday, I stopped the team and looked around. We were surrounded by huge holes in the ice, rivers of open water, and it was raining. Land was still over 100 miles away and, for the first time, I felt sure we were never going to get off the ice. We were going to die out here, cold and alone.

I didn't want us to just vanish; I wanted to leave something behind. I took out my camera, placed it in front of us on a tripod, set the timer, and climbed on the sled. This would be our final picture. Someplace just ahead we would all go through the ice. There would be no one to help us and, together, we would sink to the bottom of Queen Maud Gulf.

I took the picture and then tied the camera to my sled. The camera was waterproof and I hoped that one day someone might find it, look at the picture, and figure out what had happened to us.

The ice was breaking up fast but Anna bravely led us forward, jumping from one chunk of ice to the next. The dogs were fearless as they leaped across cracks more than three feet wide. June 6 passed in a blur of slush, water, and exhaustion. King William Island finally appeared on the horizon and drew us like a magnet through twenty exhausting hours. On June 7 we reached the edge of the ice. Between us and the shores of King William Island was over 100 yards of open water and no way to cross.

"Haw, Anna!" I called. Anna turned left and we sledded along the edge of the ice, searching for some way to reach land.

There were many holes in the ice but the standing water made them difficult to see. I had just glanced away toward the land when I heard a huge splash. I looked back at the team and Anna was gone!

She had fallen through one of the holes! She swam back up to the surface and thrust her front paws onto the ice. Anna struggled to lift herself out of the freezing water but the ice was too slick and she couldn't get a grip. I ran up and grabbed her by the harness and started to lift. But the ice around the hole was so thin it began breaking away under me. If I fell into the water, we might both drown. I had to let go of Anna's harness.

She fell back into the water.

I ran back to the sled and called "Douggie, haw!"

Douggie pulled left and tried to drag her out. But he was too weak.

"Douggie! Haw! Haw!" I yelled.

Douggie kept pulling and Anna kept clawing at the ice. Together they tried with all their might, but they were not strong enough.

Anna's eyes were huge with terror. The water was freezing cold. She couldn't hold out much longer. I had to do something now!

In a panic I screamed, "Douggieeeee! Haaaaaw!!!"

This time, the other dogs understood what had to happen. All seven dogs turned to the left and all seven dogs pulled. Anna dug her toenails into the ice. The dogs pulled, Anna lifted. They kept pulling and pulling. Anna kept lifting and lifting. Together they used every ounce of strength they had.

And this time was different. This time, it was enough. This time, Anna was pulled out of the water.

For a moment we all stood there on the ice, no one moving, no one making a sound. We were all still alive, we were all still a team. I wanted to hug every one of those dogs but there was no time. We had to keep moving and get off the ice before we all fell through.

I thought Anna might be too frightened to go on, but I was wrong. She stood up, shook herself off, and went back to work as though this sort of thing happened every day. Once again, I was filled with enormous respect for my courageous little dog.

After that our luck changed. About fifteen minutes later, we found a tiny peninsula that stuck out into the gulf and we were able to sled up onto land. I dropped to my knees and kissed the ground and then I gave each dog a very big hug.

We stayed on King William Island in the small village of Gjoa Haven for the next five and a half months, living with the Qitsualik family, kind and generous Inuit people. On

December 5, the sun set for the winter. It would not rise again for six weeks but the sea ice was once again thick enough to travel on, so I said good-bye to my adopted family and we left Gjoa Haven in the pale dawn light of a sun that never rose.

Over the next 500 miles, we sledded among vast, rolling hills, crossed bays blocked with massive piles of broken ice, struggled up rivers choked with giant boulders and almost no ice, and managed to stay warm in temperatures down to fifty-six degrees below zero. No matter the challenges, we overcame them all.

On January 9, after sledding 2,500 miles across arctic wilderness, we reached our destination of Repulse Bay. Watching the dogs as they rested on the beach that day, I felt enormous pride. All those naysayers who said we would fail—they were all wrong. They were wrong about Anna. She wasn't too small. She had done extremely well and had emerged as a gifted, confident, single lead dog. Anna was a hero.

They were wrong about all my dogs. Every dog had played an important role in accomplishing what we had set out to do. When things got tough, we didn't give up. We pulled together as a team and found a way to keep going every single time. My team was worthy of respect and they were all heroes. Not bad for "a bunch of clunkers."

8

ENOUGH

Sojo stood in her harness with her head turned to the left as far as it could possibly go. She did this every time I hooked up my dog team. The reason for her behavior was simple: her brother Roald was barking directly into her right ear again, the way he did every time I put him in harness. It must have hurt Sojo's ear but she never stood up to him and she suffered his annoying behavior in silence. When I was a kid my brother used to harass me endlessly, so I knew how she felt. I hoped Sojo would learn to stand up for herself better than I had.

"Roald!" I shouted, "Knock it off."

He stopped barking but then began playfully bumping Sojo with his shoulder. Clearly Roald thought this was all in good fun and I don't think he had any idea how unpleasant this was for Sojo. Another shout from me and Roald straightened up and finally left Sojo alone.

A few times I had tried moving Roald to different places in the team to give Sojo a break but that only made things worse. While I hooked up the other dogs, Roald would bark and bark and lunge toward Sojo as if to say, *Hey, Sojo! I'm over here. I'm over here.* The other dogs were not so tolerant of his foolishness and whoever was next to him would bark angrily trying to get him to shut up.

To keep the peace, I always ended up moving Roald back beside Sojo. I knew Roald had little confidence and acting out was his way of avoiding what made him feel the least bit stressed. I hoped with Sojo's patience and my corrections, Roald would learn to calm down and feel less anxiety.

By the time I decided to dogsled 2,500 miles across the Arctic, Sojo and Roald were part of my eight-dog team. Both dogs worked hard but they were only a year old and I was still a little worried that they might be too young for such a long and difficult journey. The only way to find out was to go north to the Arctic to train and see how they did.

As the weeks of training went by, Sojo gained more skill as a sled dog. She learned to slow down through rough ice, when to pull hard, and when to stop and wait for my command. I was impressed. In camp she seemed able to forget about Roald's bad behavior and often wrestled around with him before snuggling down for the night. I felt confident that Sojo was capable of going on the expedition. But brother Roald was still a question.

One day during training we encountered some very rough sledding. Pieces of ice three feet across and six inches thick lay piled across our path like slabs of demolished concrete. The farther we went the worse the ice got. Getting through this stuff was going to be difficult and tricky.

When I gave a command to go left around a big chunk of ice, Sojo went left with the other dogs but Roald hesitated and then stopped. Sojo tugged left as if to say, *Come on, Roald. Come this way.* Sojo continued following commands as we weaved our way through the ice and with every command she patiently gave Roald a little tug.

Roald watched Sojo very carefully and tried to do everything she did but he wasn't pulling. If he refused to pull in rough ice I would have to drop him from the team. Finally, after about a half hour of Sojo's constant encouragement, Roald finally began pulling. An hour later we emerged onto smooth ice.

"Yahoo!" I cheered, "We made it!"

I was thrilled by what had happened back there. Sojo and Roald had begun working as their own little team and had made it through. This was the kind of progress I was looking for and now I was confident they both were ready for the expedition.

I threw my head back and howled with joy. "Wooooooo."

With tails wagging, all the dogs pointed their noses

toward the sky and joined me in a pack howl. "Woooooo. Wooooo."

This so excited Roald, he turned and barked right into Sojo's ear. Poor Sojo turned her face away, looked out over the ice, and sighed as though to say, *Thanks a lot, bro. That's what I get for helping you?*

I was hoping that as Roald's confidence grew he would stop barking in Sojo's ear but he didn't. As the days went by, this constant harassment began to take its toll on Sojo. When I gave a command to turn left or right, Sojo turned more slowly than the other dogs. During rest breaks, she seldom fully relaxed. If Roald appeared uncertain about what to do, she no longer made an effort to help him. In camp, she stopped playing with Roald and did her best to ignore him. Worst of all, whenever Roald barked in her ear, instead of just turning her head away, she cowered from him by lowering herself to the ground. Sojo's confidence was slipping and I was getting worried about her. Somehow I had to help Sojo stand up to her brother.

I thought about the problem and formed a plan. During rest breaks I always walked along beside the team, stroking each dog and murmuring words of encouragement. I decided to change that routine. From now on, I petted Sojo first and talked softly to her. Then I moved to the front of the team and worked my way back to the sled, giving Sojo twice the attention the other dogs received. Dogs notice things like that and I was hoping it would boost Sojo's sagging morale.

After two weeks of no improvement, I was beginning to despair that the problem would ever be solved. I decided that if Roald didn't straighten up, I would drop him from the team. Then one morning things changed. When Roald moved over to bark in her ear, Sojo didn't turn her head. Instead, she stood her ground and looked straight ahead, completely ignoring him. Roald barked a couple more times but Sojo didn't bat an eye. Roald stood looking at her with his head cocked sideways. I guess it wasn't any fun if he couldn't get a reaction.

After that, there was a two-week standoff between Sojo and Roald. While I hooked up the team each morning, they stood beside each other in awkward silence. Then, early one frosty morning, just as we were preparing to leave, Roald couldn't restrain himself any more. He eased over to Sojo, ready to bark in her ear. She turned and looked him straight in the eye as if to say, *Don't you even **think** about it.*

Roald wagged his tail and opened his mouth to bark. Sojo took a step toward Roald and glared at him. *I'm warning you,* her eyes said. It was one small step for a dog but one giant step in their relationship. That one little step meant Sojo was challenging Roald. He did not bark.

Later that day we came upon an abandoned shipwreck on a remote beach. This was too exciting for me to pass up, so we stopped. While I explored the wreck, the dogs enjoyed basking in the afternoon sun. The rest made Roald feel pretty chipper, and just as we were ready to leave, he leaned over and barked in Sojo's ear. She turned and barked angrily right in his face as if to say, *I'm warning you one last time! Stop it!*

Roald was stunned. He looked at her with his mouth slightly open as if to ask, *Wow! How come you did that?*

Obviously Sojo was reaching the end of her tolerance. The situation was tense and I was worried that Sojo and Roald might get into a nasty fight. An injured dog was the last thing we needed in the middle of the arctic wilderness. As we sledded away in silence, I hoped Sojo's defiance might have taught Roald a lesson.

But the next morning, just as we were preparing to leave camp, Roald leaned over and blasted right into Sojo's ear, "Bark!"

Sojo spun around and threw herself at Roald's ear.

"Bark! Bark!" she screamed.

Roald backed up, his eyes bugged out and his mouth gaped open.

"Bark! Bark! Bark!" Sojo screamed again.

Roald turned his head and tried to pull away, but Sojo kept crowding him and shoved her mouth tight against his ear.

"Bark! Bark! Bark! Bark!"

Roald lunged to his right. But it was no use. He couldn't get away.

"Bark! Bark! Bark! Bark! Bark!"

In desperation, Roald fell over on his side. With his tongue hanging out the side of his panting mouth, he lay motionless at Sojo's feet. Sojo straddled Roald with her front legs and looked down on him, as if daring him to move so much as one muscle.

Roald's ear must have been ringing and he shook his head.

"Bark!!!"

No more head shaking. Roald lay perfectly still in a show of total dog submission.

Sojo raised her head in triumph and stared out over the tundra as though Roald didn't even exist. The team and I stood in stunned silence. The only sound was Sojo panting.

After a couple of minutes, Sojo moved over and let Roald get up. A few days later, Sojo and Roald were back to wrestling around in camp. They had worked out their problem and were friends once more.

Roald learned that if you push someone far enough, sooner or later, they will push you back. He never again barked in Sojo's ear. She showed him and us that you can stand up for yourself and still live together in peace. It's a good lesson for us humans, too. When you are getting badgered by someone and you feel angry, you don't have to fight, you don't have to throw things, you don't have to say mean and hurtful words. But you can stand up and make it clear you're not going to take it anymore—just like Sojo did.

9

GOOD-BYE, MY FRIEND

It's final. There's no going back. There's no changing anything. And it only happens to the lucky. Fate provides you
with an opportunity to look into the eyes of a dog you have
never met before and, for reasons you can't explain, you know
that dog is different from every other dog you have ever
known. Then, as if being swept along by a powerful current,
you find yourself going through life with that dog as your
best friend.

Like all good friends my dog gave me many gifts in her
life. Her greatest gift was to teach me the lesson we all must
learn: how to say good-bye when your someone dies.

Our life together started when I went to look at a litter of
sled dog puppies that were being offered for sale. This was an
exciting day because a sled dog puppy was exactly what I
needed to help me fulfill my dream of becoming a dog

musher. I scooped up one of the little fuzz balls into my arms and scratched her floppy, gray ears.

The puppy relaxed against my arm and stared straight into my eyes as if to say, *You're here! Finally! I knew you were coming.*

And that was it. I paid the owner and took the puppy home. I named her Amy because "Amy" means love and that's what I was already feeling for this puppy. That day marked the beginning of a friendship that would last nearly sixteen years.

Our days were spent almost entirely together. We ate at the same time, went on errands together, took walks, and played fetch. Every afternoon we spent time lying on the floor, quietly staring into each other's eyes. Amy had incredibly intelligent eyes and would look at me as though she were examining my innermost thoughts while I was trying to understand hers. There were no demands, no expectations, and no fear. It was a time of total acceptance and trust.

The next year I moved to Alaska, got some real sled dogs, and became a dog musher. I tried to include Amy on the team but she was a complete mess. Every time I put her in harness she would bounce all over the place. On the trail she tried to chase moose or fox and pulled as little as possible. After two seasons of nonstop antics, I had to drop Amy from the team. However, she was an outstanding mother and made a very important contribution to the team: the following spring Amy gave birth to a litter of puppies. Every single one of

them grew up to be a confident, intelligent, and hardworking sled dog.

I've always been pretty sappy when it comes to dogs and every dog I ever knew easily won a place in my heart. I decided early on in my career as a dog musher that I would keep all my dogs for their entire lives. Caring for a dozen dogs at one time brought lots of fun and immense joy into my life but it was never easy dealing with their deaths.

Most of my dogs lived twelve to fifteen years and each dog was honored with a simple, silent funeral. The dog's body was placed on a sled and dragged slowly through the dog lot, with a brief pause beside each of its teammates. The dog and I would then make our final journey together to a clearing in the forest where the burial took place.

I don't believe dogs know death is coming but, when it happens, I think they understand that something has changed forever. When we humans lose someone we care about, we need time to grieve. So do dogs. But, perhaps because their lives are so short, dogs usually don't grieve for very long. The day after a funeral my dogs were always ready to go back to living their lives.

The lesson my dogs taught me about death and dying was simple: you mourn the loss but you don't grieve forever. You move on with the living.

To support myself and my team, I earned a good living as a registered respiratory therapist. It was satisfying work but after a few years I wanted to spend more time dog mushing. So, I changed careers and became a traveling storyteller, and later a children's book author. I toured the Lower 48 states for three or four months at a time, visiting schools and libraries. This gave me more free time with my dogs.

Whenever I'd go off on tour, I would hire someone to care for my sled dogs at home. Those dogs were used to being tied up but Amy wasn't, so she always stayed with my friend Alice.

A few days before I was to leave on my second tour, Amy and I went for our evening walk. It was a beautiful calm night but there was a chill in the air so we didn't go far. On the way home, as Amy walked ahead of me, she staggered slightly and then abruptly stopped. She lowered her head and let out a low, coarse, yelp, the sound a dog makes when it feels sudden and terrible pain. We both froze in place. After a few seconds, Amy turned her head and looked at me. For the first time in her life I saw fear and confusion in her eyes.

I wanted to believe that what had just happened wasn't really important, but I knew better. The next day, the vet told me that Amy had a tumor in her abdomen and that it was inoperable. She couldn't be fixed. The weight of those words was staggering and I had to grab hold of the examining table to keep from collapsing. *How could this be happening? How could this possibly be true?*

The vet was silent for a few seconds, then he spoke quietly, "Nature can take her at any time. But that's been true her entire life."

I was angry. I felt like telling him to shut up. My best friend had just been given a death sentence and I didn't care what anybody had to say about anything.

We went home where I slumped into a chair and cried

and cried. When I finally stopped crying, I sat there in silence, thinking, *Amy is my best friend and she is not going to die. Nothing will change. I'll go on tour, Amy will stay with Alice, and she'll be waiting for me when I come home.*

So I left on tour. Every few days I called Alice.

"How's Amy?" I'd ask.

"She's fine. We go for walks every day," Alice would answer.

Over the next three months the report was always the same: everything was fine.

But about two weeks before the tour ended, when I made my usual call, Alice's report was not so reassuring.

"Amy's not eating much. Her nose is dry and she seems uncomfortable," she told me.

"Should I come home?" I asked.

"No," she said, "I think she'll be okay until you get home."

A week later, while I was in Washington State, Alice's report was more alarming. "Amy won't eat, no matter what I offer her."

"Is she drinking any water?" I asked.

"Just a little," replied Alice.

It was the same path most of my dogs had followed as they neared their death. I knew I could no longer deny that Amy was dying. I cancelled the last few days of my tour and headed home. But I had to drive over 2,000 miles to get there, which would take me three days. That first day I drove until I couldn't stay awake, napped, then drove on all night.

At noon of the second day I called Alice again. "How's she doing?" I asked.

"She's fading but I think she can hang on until you get here. Come as fast as you can," Alice told me.

All that day as I sped north, I sent thoughts to Amy, willing her to stay alive so we could see each other one more time.

Late that evening I stopped and called Alice again. Before speaking she took in a deep breath and let out a long, ragged sigh. Then she was silent. I wanted that silence to last forever because as long as there was silence I could keep clinging to the hope that Amy was still alive.

But it was not to be. In a choked voice, Alice said, "Amy died at 4:30 this afternoon."

Sometimes pain is so deep, you can't even feel it. In a calm voice, completely devoid of emotion, I heard myself thank Alice for all she had done for Amy. Then I hung up the phone. I don't know how long I sat alone beside the highway with nearly unbearable thoughts swirling through my mind.

This isn't how it was supposed to end. Amy was supposed to wait for me. We were supposed to look into each other's eyes one more time. We were supposed to have time to say good-bye. We were supposed to have a funeral and make our final journey together.

Suddenly, I was full of anger and I pounded my fist on the steering wheel. "Why didn't you wait for me?" I screamed. "How could you die without me?"

Of course it wasn't Amy's fault. It wasn't anybody's fault. It was just Amy's time to die. My emotions gave way and I cried harder than I have ever cried in my entire life.

The third day, as I drove along the highway, I paid my respects to Amy's life by thinking about the incredible journey we had made together and what a great friendship we had shared.

And I remembered what the vet had told me: "Nature can take her at anytime. But that's been true her entire life." I finally understood the meaning of those words. Those nearly sixteen years that Amy and I had spent together—every day had been a gift.

Late that afternoon I pulled into Alice's driveway. I got out of my van and walked to the grave Alice had dug. It was beside the grave of Amy's best friend, Chinook. There was fresh dirt piled beside it—Alice hadn't filled it in yet because

she wanted me to have the chance to see Amy one last time and to say good-bye.

Alice came out to join me and we stood together in silence. I was too sad to cry anymore.

Alice lowered her head and said, "I'm sorry, Pam."

At the bottom of the grave Amy was lying on her left side. As I looked down at her, I thought about the gift of friendship she had given me and I felt so deeply grateful for all we had shared.

Dogs have taught me so much about death and dying and I knew not to linger. I knew Amy would want me to grieve, but not for too long. She would want me to move on with my life because that's what dogs do. I knelt beside her grave and whispered a soft "Good-bye, Amy." And then, to honor her as a dog, I gave Amy one last gift. I let my best friend go.

10

THE GIFT OF
FORGIVENESS

This is the story of two puppies born in Alaska. One was black, the other white. One was repeatedly given away, the other thrown away. When they finally met, the black dog had a happy life, but the white dog knew only betrayal. This is the story of how these two puppies met and became friends and helped each other live happy lives.

The white puppy, a chow-Samoyed mix, was named Kaiya and she was strong-willed. Almost from the start, Kaiya had behavior problems and was given away to one person after another. By the time she was just six months old, Kaiya had already been through three homes.

About the time Kaiya was trying to fit in with her third owner, a litter of black, Lab-mix puppies was born. Four weeks later someone put the puppies into a small box, dropped them off alongside a gravel road, and drove away.

Fortunately, someone found the puppies and took them to the Alaska Dog and Puppy Rescue in Wasilla, Alaska, where volunteer Rhonda Weinrick took over their care. She bottle-fed them every four hours, around the clock, and provided everything they needed. Word spread and the sad story of the box puppies appeared in the local news.

After reading a newspaper story about them, I drove to Rhonda's house to take a look at the little celebrities. Inside the garage were seven little bundles of energy tearing around. One female skidded to a halt, sat down, and lowered her head, showing good dog manners.

"Isn't that cute," I said.

Rhonda knew how to get people to adopt puppies. She picked her up, placed her in my arms, and said with a big smile, "Here, hold her for awhile."

The puppy looked at me and yawned in my face. The scent of puppy breath drifted into my nose and melted my heart.

I named her Ellie and when she was six weeks old I took her home. The first thing I did was put Ellie in a pen beside my desk so we could be together while I worked. As we began our life together, Ellie and I were happy. But there was one problem. If I left the room for even a second, she would panic and cry nonstop until I returned. Somewhere inside that little head was the memory of being in a box beside a road. For Ellie, fear of abandonment was very real.

I knew I needed to build her trust, so I developed a routine centered around her. Every hour we went outside so she could relieve herself and we could play together. Patience, compassion, and forgiveness were the rule. If I went into another room, I picked her up and took her with me. If Ellie had an accident inside, there was no scolding. I just cleaned it up.

By three months of age Ellie was old enough to be out of her pen full-time. She followed me around our house everywhere I went—into the kitchen, the dining room, my bedroom, even the bathroom. As long as we were together, everything was fine. But if I left her in my van while I went into the grocery store, she still flew into a panic and cried until I returned. It was heartbreaking and I didn't know how to help her.

Kaiya, the white puppy, was living with her third owner, a woman named Randi, who had never owned a dog before. With the optimism of the inexperienced, Randi was sure Kaiya could be made over into a well-behaved dog. It would just take some time and a lot of love. Of course it wasn't going to be that easy. Kaiya had already been betrayed by two people and she didn't trust anyone.

One of the first things Randi did was take Kaiya to a picnic. People were gathered around the picnic table, laughing and talking, and the table was loaded with delicious food. No one was ready for what happened next.

In a single bound, Kaiya leaped onto the table! Angry voices shouted "Get down! Get off the table!" In a blur she ran through the potato salad, knocked over a bowl of peas, and made a lunge for the hamburgers.

"Somebody grab that dog!" But before anyone could stop her, Kaiya snatched a mouthful of burgers, leaped off the table, and scrambled under a nearby bush where she devoured her prize.

It's not easy living in a small community with a known troublemaker. People didn't want Kaiya around, particularly when food was present. Worse than stealing food, Kaiya fought with every dog she met.

Ellie was now six months old but she still had the energy of a six-week-old puppy.

As she tore across the front yard chasing her ball for about the fiftieth time, I said "Ellie, you need a dog friend to run off some of that energy."

Later that day I posted a sign on the post office bulletin board that read,

My dog is looking for a playmate.

I have a 25 X 50 foot pen.

For a good time, please call *******

Randi called the next day. She said she was hoping that if Kaiya could spend some time playing with another dog and develop a friendship, she might learn to trust other dogs and not fight. At first I wasn't sure I wanted a dog like Kaiya around. I was worried she might attack Ellie. At the same time I was impressed that Randi was trying to give Kaiya a chance to mend her ways, so I decided they could come over for a visit.

But there would be rules.

"We both have to stay with the dogs during the entire visit," I explained to Randi over the phone. "The dogs will meet outside the pen first so neither feels trapped. They have to wear leashes but we won't hold the leashes. That way the dogs will feel in control of their bodies. If Kaiya goes after Ellie, we'll both grab a leash and then Kaiya has to leave."

Randi agreed.

The next day Randi and Kaiya showed up on time. Ellie was relaxing on the grass chewing a large bone. When Ellie saw Kaiya, she wanted to play so she dropped down with her forelegs on the ground in a play bow. Kaiya raised her hackles. Ellie pulled back her lips in a big doggie smile. Kaiya lowered her head and growled. Ellie cocked her head and wagged her tail as if to say, *Don't you want to play?*

Then Kaiya made a lunge for Ellie's throat!

Ellie ran away to the other end of the yard and looked

back at Kaiya as if to ask, *What'd you do that for?*

Randi yelled, "Kaiya! No!" She grabbed Kaiya's leash, dragged her to the car, and left.

I was stunned and angry. Ellie had done nothing to deserve being attacked. Randi called later and asked, "You don't want us to come back, do you?"

My first reaction was to tell her "no" but after a little thought I said, "Ellie wasn't hurt and I think she would give Kaiya another chance. Bring her back in a couple of days and we'll see what happens."

The second meeting was worse. Ellie was in the front yard chewing on a bone again when Kaiya and Randi arrived. Ellie held no grudge and was happy to see Kaiya again. Ellie leaped to her feet and ran up to the car, wagging her tail.

Kaiya glared through the window at Ellie. Randi opened the car door but before she could get hold of Kaiya's collar, the dog leaped from the car and charged Ellie! Kaiya drove her face so hard into the side of Ellie's head, she knocked her over onto her back.

Randi and I were both screaming, "Kaiya! No! No! No!"

Kaiya snatched up Ellie's bone and chewed on it like she hadn't eaten in a week. Ellie was stunned. She stood up and gently shook her head. She looked confused as she walked away. I was impressed that Ellie wasn't drawn into a fight, that she was willing to let bygones be bygones.

I, however, saw things differently. My job was to protect Ellie. As Randi drove away, I decided Kaiya was too dangerous and was no longer welcome.

I was quite surprised when, a few days later, Randi called and said, "I think bones are the issue. What if we take away all the bones and try again?"

By then my anger had faded. I looked at Ellie standing beside me. She wanted a friend and she always seemed ready to forgive Kaiya's bad manners. Though I was reluctant to have Kaiya come back, I decided she could have one last chance.

When Kaiya and Randi showed up again, every bone was gone from the yard. Ellie may be a forgiving dog but she wasn't a fool. Instead of running up to greet Kaiya, she stood back and waited while Kaiya sniffed around searching for a bone. Finding nothing, Kaiya raised her head and looked around as though she was wondering what to do next. Then the most amazing thing happened. Both dogs dropped their front ends in a play bow and began chasing each other in a huge circle around the yard. It was as if they had both decided to cross some invisible line together and form a silent truce.

As I watched them playing, I felt proud of Ellie. If she hadn't been willing to forgive Kaiya, this would never have happened. It was a very happy day for everyone.

Over the next month, Kaiya visited Ellie many times and they had a lot of fun. Of course, much more was happening than just two dogs having fun. In our yard, Kaiya found a sanctuary, a place where she could be with another dog and not be afraid. Kaiya's damaged spirit was beginning to heal.

After a couple of months we decided to reintroduce bones, but this time we had a new plan. When Randi and Kaiya arrived I said, "I put four bones around the yard. Let's see what happens"

But Kaiya's old fears bubbled up. A bone meant food, and to her that meant fighting for survival. When she saw the bones, she immediately grabbed one and began chewing. As Ellie chose a bone for herself, Kaiya leaped to her feet and charged her. Ellie dropped the bone and walked away. At this point in their relationship I believed that Ellie understood Kaiya's fear and was willing to endlessly forgive her. But I also believed that Kaiya needed to learn that her bad behavior was not acceptable and there would be consequences.

"Kaiya's not being a very nice friend today," I said to Ellie. "Let's go."

With that, we turned our backs on Kaiya and went in the house. Randi took Kaiya's bone away and drove her home. The consequence was quick and simple—if you can't be nice you lose your bone and your playtime. We did this day after day. Finally, after a month, Kaiya stopped stealing bones from Ellie. We were sure Kaiya had learned her lesson.

Over the next year, Kaiya came to visit us four or five

times a week. Whenever Randi went away, Kaiya would stay with us. Occasionally, she would steal a bone from Ellie, but Ellie always forgave her. Then one warm, sunny afternoon, things changed. Randi and I were sitting on the deck watching the dogs play. The heat soon made them tired so they each found a bone to gnaw on. After a few minutes Kaiya walked over to Ellie, snatched the bone right out of her mouth, and walked away.

Normally when this happened Ellie would look at Kaiya as if to say, *No problem, I'll find another bone.* But this time was different. Maybe it was the heat, or maybe Ellie was just tired of having her bones stolen. Instead of finding another bone, Ellie headed toward Kaiya.

I couldn't believe my eyes. I know dogs and I could tell from Ellie's determined stride that there was going to be trouble. Ellie wasn't thinking about forgiveness, she wanted her bone back. Was Ellie going to attack Kaiya? Was there going to be a fight?

Kaiya watched Ellie approaching out of the corner of her eye and raised her hackles.

Ellie kept walking.

Kaiya stopped chewing and stood up. I stood up too and called "Ellie! Come!" But she ignored me.

Kaiya put her mouth down beside the bone and growled.

Ellie didn't even slow down.

"No! Ellie, come!" I shouted. Ellie kept walking.

Kaiya's legs stiffened. She bared her teeth, snapped her jaws together, and made a nasty, frightening snarl. There was going to be a dog fight!

I ran toward the dogs. "Ellie!" I screamed. "Ellie! No! Come here! Ellie! Come!"

Ellie stopped beside her bone, her face inches from Kaiya's bared teeth.

But there was no fight. Without a curl of her lips or a growl from her throat, Ellie picked up her bone and walked off with it clenched tightly between her teeth.

Kaiya did nothing! If ever there was a look of total disbelief on a dog's face, it was on Kaiya's at that moment. Kaiya stood like a little statue watching Ellie walk away as if to say, *Hey . . . uh . . . hey wait, wait, wait. You can't do that.*

I was sure it wasn't over. I was sure Kaiya would steal that bone back.

But she didn't. Kaiya went back to gnawing her own bone again. Randi and I looked at each other in astonishment. "Did you see that?" I asked.

"Yes, I did," said Randi, her eyes wide. We burst out laughing and shook our heads in amazement.

As the weeks and months passed, the scars from their puppyhoods slowly faded. Occasionally, the dogs "borrowed" bones from one another, but they never fought.

In time, both dogs' spirits were healed by their friendship. Kaiya stopped being frightened and angry, and eventually made friends with a few other dogs. Bonding with Kaiya reconnected something in Ellie that had been broken when she was so cruelly snatched from her mother as a four-week-old puppy.

Now, when I leave Ellie in my van to go into the grocery store, she doesn't panic and cry anymore. Thanks to her friendship with Kaiya, Ellie is no longer afraid of being abandoned.

11

THE DAY A POLAR BEAR CAME VISITING

I f there hadn't been another person with me to act as my witness, no one would ever believe this story. But it's true, every word. This journey would test the courage of me and my dogs beyond anything I ever imagined.

My dog mushing friend Kate and I departed the tiny Canadian arctic community of Resolute Bay with the idea of dog sledding to the Magnetic North Pole. It was only 325 miles and would take a couple of weeks. We both loved being in the Arctic and were looking forward to what we thought would be a fun and easy trip.

Twice in our journey we were pinned down by blizzards, but Kate and I were old hands at arctic travel and knew the drill. Before the storm engulfs you, cover all supplies with a tarp so you can find them when the storm ends. Next, flip the sleds on their sides to shelter the dogs from the wind and set up the tent. Finally, snuggle into your sleeping bag, sip hot tea, check on the dogs from time to time, read a good book, and wait.

By the end of the tenth day, we had gone about 250 miles and were only about 75 miles away from the Magnetic North Pole. It was a breezy day and we had sledded through some nasty ice piled up nearly to our shoulders. Happily for us, as evening approached the wind let up and we came to flat ice covered by a few inches of wind-packed snow. It was a good place to camp so Kate and I decided to stop for the day.

As I climbed off my sled, I was struck by the beauty around us. To the north, south, and east the ice extended for seemingly endless miles. About a mile to the west were low-lying mountains completely barren of trees. I could see no wildlife but we had noticed many tracks in the snow. I knew the area was home to arctic hare, fox, caribou, and a few species of birds, and I knew that polar bears roamed the ice hunting seals.

Kate and I took out our snowhooks (big iron hooks attached to the sled by a heavy line) and jammed them into the snow. These hooks would hold our teams in place so they couldn't run off without us. The dogs curled up to rest while Kate and I worked to set up camp. Even though it was late, we didn't need our headlamps because we were above the Arctic Circle where the sun never sets in April.

After we got the tent set up, Kate and I crawled inside to lay out our sleeping bags and stove. Then we began the three-hour process of melting snow in a five-gallon bucket to make water for the dogs.

"Wow, it's almost ten at night. No wonder I'm so tired."

"It's been a long day but we're making really good time," Kate answered. "Two more days and we should be at the Magnetic North Pole."

"Do you think we'll have any problem with bears?"

Kate, a biologist, shrugged, "If we do see one, it will likely be at a distance. They usually avoid people."

The warmth from the stove was making us drowsy. Except for the soft hiss of the stove, it was silent. My eyelids drooped and I fell asleep sitting up.

"Woof, woof, woof!" The silence was shattered by the dogs barking in alarm!

"Woof, woof, woof!"

Kate and I looked at each other wide-eyed. We knew the only thing that could cause such uproar around here was a fox or polar bear.

I scrambled over to the tent door on my hands and knees and looked outside. The dogs were lunging in their harnesses toward something behind the tent. I stuck my head around the corner of the tent to see what they were barking at.

A polar bear bounded past me so close its fur almost brushed across my nose!

I jerked back inside the tent. "Did you see that?"

Kate could only nod her head.

"That bear walked right past me!" I said, still trying to grasp what had just happened.

Kate squeaked, "Uh huh."

I poked my head out again and what I saw shocked me even more. The bear was standing in front of Kate's team and sniffing her lead dog's face! The frightened dog turned its head to avoid eye contact with the bear. The bear sniffed the dog's neck. The dog quickly lowered itself to the snow in a display of total submission.

The bear leaned over the dog and opened its mouth.

I scrambled outside and grabbed my shotgun.

As I stood up, the bear jerked its head up and looked straight at me. It was a female, maybe six feet long from tail to nose. I raised the shotgun to my shoulder, held my breath, and took careful aim at the bear's neck.

But I didn't shoot. The bear stood between me and Kate's dogs. If I shot and missed, one of Kate's dogs might be killed. Firing a shot now was too great a risk, so I waited for the bear to move away from the dogs.

Kate crawled out of the tent and stood beside me. Unfortunately, her shotgun was still on her sled. To get it she would have to go too close to the bear. Kate was defenseless. Very slowly I moved over one step, placing myself between the bear and Kate and waited for the bear to move.

The dogs were calming down a little and were no longer lunging at the bear, but they were still barking. By contrast, the bear was calm and stood silently, swinging its gaze from the dogs to me and back to the dogs. She ambled along Kate's team, sniffing each dog, but always keeping an eye on me.

As she walked past Kate's sled, I had a clear shot. Again, I hesitated. The whiteness of her fur told me she was very young, maybe just a two-year-old. She was displaying the behavior of a curious dog. She had almost certainly never seen a human or a dog in her life and probably just wanted to know what we were. It didn't feel right to shoot her.

When the bear approached my lead dog, Jocko, I was terrified. But when the bear sniffed Jocko's face, the most amazing thing happened. Jocko fell silent, lay down, and curled up on the snow as though he was going to sleep. All at once, every dog followed Jocko's example. They laid down and tucked their noses under their tails. But they were not sleeping—all eyes stayed wide open, watching the bear's every move.

The bear walked slowly along my team, stopping to sniff each dog. With the bear distracted, Kate and I edged over to her sled and grabbed her shotgun. She flipped off the safety and whispered, "What should we do?"

"Nothing," I said in a low voice. "I think this is a young bear just turned out by her mother. I think she's just curious. If we give her a chance, she might just leave."

Kate raised her eyebrows and took a deep breath. In a not very convincing voice, she said, "I hope you're right."

The bear had reached my sled and began rummaging around, using her paw to pull out one object at a time. First out was a burlap bag filled with seventy pounds of frozen, ground chicken. With a single swipe of her paw, the bear ripped the bag open and scattered chicken across the snow. Apparently chicken wasn't on the bear's menu and she ate none of it. She turned her attention back to my sled and continued entertaining herself by tossing out my spare socks and making a general mess.

Finding nothing edible, the bear eyed my dog Hank, who lay curled up right in front of my sled. She lumbered over and sniffed the top of his head. Hank very slowly raised himself into a sitting position, curled back his lips, and made a throaty growl through clenched teeth, "Grrrrr."

Hank could see he was in a very tough spot. If he attacked the bear, he probably would be killed. If the bear attacked Hank, I would shoot her. But if I didn't kill her with one shotgun shell, she would turn and attack me and I would be killed.

The bear opened her mouth wide and placed her teeth on the back of Hank's neck. Hank did not appreciate this.

"Grrrr," he growled again.

With agonizing slowness, the bear moved her mouth along Hank's spine as though testing to see what he was. In an extraordinary display of courage and restraint, Hank remained rigid. Only his eyes rolled back toward the bear as he growled again.

It was gut-wrenching trying to decide what to do. But I still thought it best to let the bear satisfy her curiosity and hope that she would move on from Hank.

Apparently Hank wasn't on the bear's menu either, so she headed back to my sled. After a few more minutes of poking around my gear, she slowly ambled away from our camp. When she got about 200 feet away from us and seemed to have lost interest, Kate and I looked at each other and sighed with relief.

"Guess she's had enough," I said.

Of course I had spoken too soon. Just as those words left my mouth, the bear stopped and turned back. Our brief respite was eclipsed by what the bear did next. Apparently a five-foot-tall, green tent with a pointed top was too much to ignore. Who knew? Our hearts sank as the bear trotted back.

When she reached our tent, she stood on her hind legs, grabbed the top with her teeth, and pulled it over. Stakes flew everywhere and we heard the ugly sound of fabric tearing. Then she jumped up and down on the tent, dragged it around, and shook it with her teeth like a puppy playing with a new toy. Unfortunately, that "toy" was our only shelter. Finally, to our great dismay, she then used her four-inch claws to shred the tent to ribbons.

In a cold, stony voice I said, "It's time to set limits."

"Okay. Just exactly how far do we let her go?" Kate asked.

"We need our parkas to survive and we need our radio-phone to call for a rescue plane if she hurts us or a dog. So, if she starts to damage our parkas or radio, we have to shoot her," I replied.

Once she had demolished the tent, the bear raised her head slightly and shifted her eyes to me. Polar bears might look cute and cuddly in books or on TV, but when you are standing face-to-face with one and it has just trashed your tent and supplies, it doesn't look so cute anymore. A polar bear's face shows almost no emotion. They just stare directly at you with their coal-black eyes. The bear slowly, deliberately started walking straight toward me. A wave of panic washed over me.

The bear was only fifteen feet away from me when she stopped.

"Do you want me to shoot?" asked Kate, her voice urgent.

I wanted desperately to say, "Yes, kill the bear." Now I knew how my dogs felt when the bear walked so close to them. I also knew that if Kate shot and missed, the bear would attack me and I would almost certainly die. I needed to stay calm and show the same courage my dogs had shown. In the most terrifying, uncertain moment of my entire life, I answered firmly, "No, don't shoot."

"Are you sure?" asked Kate, incredulously.

I wasn't sure of anything. I was so afraid, it was hard to breathe, hard to think.

Does fear smell? Does the bear smell my fear? Stop being afraid, Pam. Put your fear away. Get in control. Think!

"Don't shoot," I repeated, trying to sound calm. "Her body language is still like a curious dog. Give her every chance to go away." I hoped with all my being that I was right.

At that moment, the bear settled back a bit on her feet and seemed to relax. It was as though she somehow understood that we didn't want to harm her. Once again, I thought maybe she would leave.

But then the most extraordinary event I have ever witnessed in the Arctic began to unfold.

The bear turned from me to the sled and it seemed to me that her eyes widened just a tiny bit. My dogs raised their heads and followed the bear with their eyes as she trotted to the back of my sled. The bear looked the handlebar up and down and then peeked around the sled at my dogs. All at once the dogs leaped to their feet and started barking. This is exactly what they do when they think I'm going to take them for a run.

The bear seized her opportunity!

In a flash, she stood up on her hind legs, grasped the handlebar with her front paws, and shook the sled! The dogs lunged forward in their harnesses. The fact that a polar bear was standing in my place seemed to make no difference whatsoever to the dogs. They were ready to go! The sled was moving! One inch, two inches . . . The snowhooks began to give way!

My team was breaking free with a polar bear driving them!

Fortunately, before they could get far, the bear's inexperience as a dog musher proved her undoing. When the sled jerked forward, she lost her balance and fell over. I grabbed my lead dogs by their harnesses and finally managed to calm everyone down. The bear stood—on four feet this time—and shook herself. Then, as though she'd had enough of the whole business, she swung around and headed out over the sea ice with her head held high. Nothing was hurt except perhaps her pride.

The entire event had been so extreme, so ridiculous, and so intense, when Kate and I looked at each other, the tension broke like a piece of brittle ice and we burst out laughing.

As we watched the bear saunter off across the ice, I looked at my watch. "It's midnight, Kate. That bear was in our camp for two hours!"

Not too far from the remains of our camp stood tall pinnacles of ice, about six to ten feet high. The young bear

approached one and, using her claws, pulled herself up to the top and then slid on her belly down the other side. She moved to the next one and the next. She was, after all, just a young curious bear out exploring her world and having fun. As Kate and I watched her disappear among the ice blocks, her white coat gleaming under the midnight sun, we were glad we had not taken her life. She had hurt no one and, as we discussed later, property damage is not a capital offense.

The restrained and courageous behavior of our dogs inspired Kate and me to stay calm during most of the bear's visit and probably saved that bear's life. Now that the excitement was over, the dogs sat staring at us, patiently waiting for their well-deserved supper.

Our tent was badly damaged but not our spirits. After surviving a long and crazy visit from a polar bear, we were not about to quit. We got out our dental floss, sewed the tent fabric back together as best we could, and continued our journey. Two days later we achieved our goal of sledding to the Magnetic North Pole. It had been the most unusual journey I have ever taken in the Arctic.

GLOSSARY

Cache: A place where provisions are placed for use later.

Come-haw: The command that requires the lead dog to turn sharply left and lead the team in the opposite direction from which it was traveling.

Commands: The words used by a musher to tell the lead dog what to do.

Dog lot: A place where dogs live, each in their own house.

Dog musher: A person that stands on the sled runners or sometimes runs alongside the sled. She is the coach, or boss, of the team, giving the dogs commands so they know where to go.

Haw: The command to turn a dog team left.

Honest dog: A term of respect for a dog that is dependable and works hard even when tired.

Hypothermia: A condition in which a body becomes too cold to maintain its normal temperature and shuts down blood flow to the hands, arms, feet, and legs in an attempt to keep warmth in the vital organs. As the body temperature drops, a person loses coordination and the ability to think clearly. If not treated, it results in freezing to death.

Gee: The command to turn a dog team right, (pronounced like the letter *g*).

Lead dog: A dog that runs in the front of the team and follows the musher's commands.

Magnetic North Pole: The location in the Northern Hemisphere where the Earth's magnetic forces enter the Earth. The Magnetic North Pole shifts constantly.

Play bow: A position assumed by a dog that shows it wants to play. The dog lowers its front legs to the ground but leaves its back end standing.

Sea ice: Ice that forms when ocean salt water freezes.

Snowhook: A heavy, two-pronged, iron hook, attached to the sled, that is used to anchor the sled by jamming the prongs into the snow.

Swing dog: The position right behind the lead dog.

Team dog: Any dog in the team except lead, swing, or wheel.

Tundra: Treeless plains of the arctic regions, with low-growing vegetation on top of cold, often frozen, soil.

Wheel dog: The position right in front of the sled.

Whoa: The command used to stop a dog team.

CPSIA information can be obtained at www.ICGtesting.com
Printed in the USA
BVOW021627090713

325054BV00004B/4/P